LIFE'S GREATEST LESSON

What I Have Learned
From The Happiest People I Know

ALLEN R. HUNT

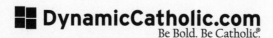
DynamicCatholic.com
Be Bold. Be Catholic®

LIFE'S GREATEST LESSON

First Edition
Copyright © 2013 Allen R. Hunt
Published by Beacon Publishing

ISBN Hard Cover: 978-1-937509-57-6
ISBN Soft Cover: 978-1-937509-58-3

The Best Version of Yourself® and
Dynamic Catholic® and Be Bold. Be Catholic.®
are registered trademarks of The Dynamic Catholic Institute.

Design by Shawna Powell & Jenny Miller

For more information on this title and other
books and CDs available through the
Dynamic Catholic Book Program, please visit:

www.DynamicCatholic.com

Printed in the United States of America.

TABLE OF CONTENTS

To

CHRISTINA

DIANNE

DOUG

GLENN

HOLLYCE

JERRY ANN

KAY

LINDA

MARK

MATTHEW

MEGGIE

MIKE

RAY

STAN

THAYER

WAYNE

The happiest,
most generous people I know

Look up to heaven,
and do not forfeit it for earth.

SAINT FRANCIS DE SALES

PROLOGUE

Something is missing. You are not whole just yet. What if you had a need in your life that turned out to be the greatest need of all? A need that you unexpectedly discovered, almost by accident? What if that need, when satisfied, grew into the most deeply rewarding aspect of your life?

You do have such a need. And when you satisfy this need, your life will be transformed in ways you could never imagine. You will never have to worry about ending your life like Ebenezer Scrooge, full of bitterness and regret. Because you will have found the cure for selfishness, for anxiety, for sluggishness, and even for anger.

That transformation will propel you toward becoming the-best-version-of-yourself. Best of all, you will lead a life full of love. You will have discovered how to get the most out of your life. You will have discoverd life's greatest lesson.

This book, and the plan that accompanies it, will show you how to do just that—how to return to the grace of who you really are.

INTRODUCTION

You learn things at funerals you would never learn anywhere else. That's because funerals bring clarity. And few people have a funeral like Mrs. Lavish Grace's. When her friends and family gathered at the funeral home and the church to celebrate her life, no one was more surprised by what happened than her grandson, ten-year-old Christopher Grace. On that unique funeral weekend, Christopher experienced things he never could have expected.

He also discovered life's greatest lesson.

This is his story.

1 : THE REASON

Do you remember the first time you touched a dead body? I do. But you have to know more before I can tell you about it. Don't worry. I'll tell you in a minute.

Oh yeah—my name's Christopher Grace, and I'm ten years old. I live in Lake Bobola, Florida, with my mom and dad and my little brother, Michael. He's only five, but I taught him to ride his bike. That tricycle thing had to go.

I'm not the biggest kid in my class, but I am the fastest. Every time we run sprints at school, I finish first. And I am the best shortstop in Florida. I like to think so anyway. Because I made the all-star team and didn't make an error all year.

Plus, I'm smart. Especially in math. It's just so easy. Mom and Dad say I'm precocious, but I don't know what that means.

By the way, Lake Bobola isn't on the beach. Most folks think every place in Florida is on the beach. Lake Bobola is in the middle of the state. We have lots of orange groves and pastures and stuff like that. It's Florida, but it's not the beach.

Anyway, my grandmother was Mrs. Lavish Grace. I called her Grandma Lavish. She was kinda short with red hair. Dad said she dyed it to keep the gray out. Maybe you knew her. If you didn't, I know you would have liked her. Everybody did.

Her life was special. I knew that way back when she told me the story about the first time she ever touched a dead body. I know that sounds weird, but it isn't.

"Christopher," Grandma Lavish said, "you know I have a sister. Your great-aunt, Jessica. We were just two years apart, so we were stuck together like Siamese twins growing up. We were never apart. She was the older sister, and I was the baby, the apple of her eye. Just like your little brother will be for you one day. And Jessica loved to teach me new stuff. Something inside her just liked to watch me learn how to do new things."

Grandma Lavish paused and smiled when she told me that. I think she had a special picture in her mind of when she and Aunt Jessica were little. Old people love that stuff. They like to remember and tell you all about when they were little. Not me. I'd much rather be grown-up. And I will be, someday. And soon, I hope.

Then Grandma Lavish started again with her story. "But touching the dead body—that story involves me and your Aunt Jessica. And it happened at the lake."

Of course, I knew all about the lake. We loved to go there. Transylvania Lake is not a huge lake like the ones tourists come to Florida to enjoy; Transylvania is just a small lake that folks in Lake Bobola like to play in on a steamy summer afternoon. Groups of cabins line the shore along with a few large homes that some lawyers in town had built to show off all their success, or at least that's what my dad says.

But most of the activity is at the beach. Dad said a long time ago the town created a big sandy spot along a stretch of shore on the lake about as long as our football field, just a place for all of us to go and have fun. On weekdays, not many folks go there. But the beach is total insanity on a Saturday or a Sunday in July when everybody in Beverley County crowds onto the beach, or on their boats and docks, to fight the heat of the Florida sun.

We still go there all the time. I love it. Me and my friends used to build castles in the sand when we were little, but now I am learning to water-ski. And I'm really good at it too. You should see me.

Anyway, Grandma Lavish kept talking. "When this story happened, Jessica was nearly eight years old and I was six, which meant I was excited about the beginning of first grade so I could go to school with all the 'big girls.'

"Our family went out to the lake for a picnic. Jessica wanted to go down to the beach. She knew that was where all the big boys and girls liked to hang out, and she wanted to be a part of that action. Of course, I also had a few friends from preschool at St. Catherine's parish, and I hoped one or two of them might be there so we could play in the sand. We weren't big enough to do much else.

"My parents, your great-grandparents, their names were Roy and Ruth Spears. You need to remember their names.

Nobody ever remembers their great-grandparents' names anymore. Well, they packed some sandwiches and toys, and set out with all of us toward the beach to enjoy a fun day in the sun along with the other families with kids in the town. There was an area shallow enough near the beach that my father could tie his little boat to a tree and leave it there while Jessica and I went to find the bliss of sand between our toes.

"Once they had tied off the boat, everything went according to plan. Mom and Dad put Jessica in charge of me, as usual, and planned to keep an eye on us from the boat as we waded out to head to the beach. Dad placed a cap over his face to hide the sun so he could lie down on the floor of the boat to snooze a bit while the gentle waves of Transylvania rocked beneath him. Mom kept watch over us girls from her seat in the boat.

"Jessica and I set up our little spot on the beach in the sea of blankets, umbrellas, and chairs. Teenagers sprinted between the sunbathers. Some boys played a halfhearted game of beach volleyball. Little girls banded together to create a princess castle in the sand, and families waded into the shallow water to seek cool relief from the heat.

"Jessica laid out her blanket, and then turned me loose to join the girls building the sand castle. What a perfect way to enjoy a late July morning.

"From the water, Haley Sneeden called out to me to come out and join her. The Sneeden family was lounging on a small boat just outside the roped-in swimming area of the lake. Haley and I had become good friends the first day of preschool at St. Catherine's.

"So, when Haley called out to me from the boat, I never batted an eye. I just leapt up from the sand castle and ran toward Haley and the Sneeden family. I ran through the shallow swimming water and then into the deeper water before I realized that my feet were no longer touching the bottom. Jessica yelled at me from the shore, telling me to stop, but I was focused like a piece of metal on a magnet, running toward Haley and the boat that floated just a few feet in front of me. I was just six. I thought I could make it. It never occurred to me that I was about to drown. Until it was too late.

"Jessica sprinted toward the water, realizing suddenly that I was not going to stop. By this time, it was too late, and I was frantically flailing my arms, trying to stay afloat. I wanted to scream, and I made the effort, but nothing came out. Can you imagine how scared I was? My little body was consumed by the effort of trying to stay afloat, and the water was filling up my mouth and throat.

"Jessica ran through the water, yelling at the surrounding swimmers. She screamed toward the Sneedens on their boat, but Mr. and Mrs. Sneeden had their backs turned to where little Haley was calling out to me, and they were oblivious to what was unfolding behind them. There was so much noise among the teenagers as they swam that only one man heard Jessica as she cried out for help in trying to save me.

"Father Frank Cascia had been swimming alone on the edge of the roped area, occasionally watching the teenagers to be sure that the young people he had brought from his parish were under control and not disrupting the other families in the water. He heard Jessica and immediately began scanning the surroundings to find the little girl, me, that Jessica was yelling for.

"This young priest swam furiously through the water, seeing my small, bobbing head as it rose and fell in the water. Jessica was little and her body didn't cooperate as she desperately tried to reach me, her precious baby sister. I think the combination of Jessica's inability to get to me and the emotional shock of realizing that she was about to lose the single most significant person in her life proved too much for that little eight-year-old.

"Father Cascia, however, was strong and capable. He had only been ordained as a priest for three years and was a rugged young man of thirty-four. Lake Bobola was his first solo assignment as a priest. It was a small town where he could develop relationships with people and learn how to lead a parish. Raised on a farm, he responded first, asked questions later. Father Cascia skimmed through the water, spotted me, and reached out and scooped up my little body. Meanwhile I was turning blue from the lack of oxygen and the cold water.

"With me in hand, Father Cascia finished the short twenty-foot swim over to the Sneedens' boat. By this time, Haley had grabbed her father, who was now anxiously watching from the edge of the boat. Father Cascia handed me up to Mr. Sneeden, and then climbed up the side of the boat himself. He laid me out on the flat surface of the boat and began to push on my little chest and breathe into my mouth.

"Jessica watched all this helplessly from the water. The desperation of the moment had paralyzed her. With every ounce of faith she could muster, my big sister prayed to God and asked that she die in place of her precious little sister, making a bargain with God in hopes of saving the one life she cared most about. Guilt washed over her. She kept asking herself how she could have not been paying attention when I ran out into the water. How could she be the one responsible for the death of her baby sister?

"After a minute or two that must have seemed like a decade to Jessica, Father Cascia began to smile. My little body wriggled like a freshly caught fish, I coughed up some water, and Mr. Sneeden shouted, 'Oh, thank God!'

"A young lifeguard assisted Jessica as she made her way to the boat to see me for herself. Somehow, God had answered Jessica's desperate prayers for mercy. I was alive. Because Father Cascia had saved me.

"Jessica climbed aboard the boat with some help from the grown-ups. The Sneedens embraced her and me both. The crowd of onlookers in the water cheered. Our parents came rushing over, frantic and stunned since they had not been able to help at all. They all tell me that I looked up at my sister and smiled the sweetest smile ever seen in Florida. I don't know about that, but I do remember being so scared at first, and then so happy to see my sister that my head was about to burst. I couldn't contain myself.

"No one was really paying attention, though, as Father Cascia moved to the other side of the boat and sat down. Everyone simply rejoiced at his heroic behavior. A six-year-old girl had been drowning and near death; now she was alive.

"Father Cascia sat down, and then placed his hand over his chest. The few folks who saw the movement thought he was just tired and relieved. He lay down on the boat seat. He made no sound; he offered no word. It took several minutes before Mrs. Sneeden realized that Father Cascia was not asleep on the deck, but that he had actually died. Mr. Sneeden turned to say thank you to the priest but quickly discovered that it looked like Father Cascia had suffered a massive heart attack. Rather than lying down for a rest, he actually had fallen into what looked like a nap but was in fact the end of his much-too-short life.

"A roller coaster of emotions swept all over the swimming area. First, the news of my tragic near-drowning brought fear, which then turned to joy when I was saved, and then finally to horror as the crowd learned that Father Cascia had died, almost certainly as a result of the effort he had exerted to save me.

"Father Cascia lay dead right there on the boat deck, his body clothed only in a tank top, a pair of blue swim trunks, and a small bracelet on his left wrist."

I stared at Grandma Lavish, waiting for the moment she had promised to tell me about.

She continued, "Father Cascia was wearing a little bracelet. And on it was just one word. LOVE."

"Did you keep that bracelet?" I asked.

"No," said Grandma Lavish, "they buried Father Cascia's body with that bracelet still on his wrist. But I knew what he had done, and I saw that bracelet. And I put the two together. Father Cascia had sacrificed his life to save me, and he had done it out of love.

"I may have just been six years old, Christopher, but I walked over to his body there on the boat. And I lay down beside him, and I wrapped my arms around him. It didn't seem real to me then. I was just six. But that was the first time I ever touched a dead body.

"Now you know why I'll always remember that."

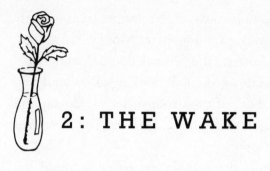

2 : THE WAKE

When I walked into the funeral home, I remembered Grandma Lavish telling me that story about Father Cascia saving her life. And I knew what I had to do. Nobody knew but me. This was going to be my first time to touch a dead body.

We arrived at the funeral home early, before all the other guests. Dad wanted us to see Grandma Lavish lying there in the casket, and he wanted us to be all by ourselves when we saw her. He thought it was important for us to have a little time before everybody else in Lake Bobola showed up and wanted to talk and visit, like they do at the funeral home whenever somebody dies.

Lake Bobola is really a small town. We don't have sky-scrapers or our own big league baseball team like Tampa. I cheer for the Tigers, like my dad does. They come to spring training not far from Lake Bobola, so we go there two or three times every March to watch them play. Dad even lets me skip school sometimes to go.

Anyway, my family got to the funeral home a little earlier than everybody else. My dad's just like that. I don't know why. He always has to be early. If he's not ten minutes early, he feels late. And when we got there, Mom and Dad got to talking to Mr. Forrest, the funeral home director, so I snuck off. I walked down the hall, looking all around that spooky old place. Lots of dark rooms, locked doors, and organ music piping in through the speakers. They even had speakers in the bathroom.

About three doors down from the office, I found the room where Grandma Lavish was. Well, it wasn't really her, I guess. Just her body. Because she was dead now. I tiptoed into the room so nobody would see me or stop me. Nobody else was in there. That's when something just came over me. A feeling I couldn't control. Like it was bubbling up from down inside my belly. I just had to know: What does a dead person feel like? I had no choice but to touch her. Not to be mean or to make a mess or to steal something. Just to touch her. So I would know—what a dead person feels like.

There she was, seventy-one years old. Lying on her back with her hands crossed over her stomach. She wore that pretty yellow flower dress she used to love to wear at Easter. That made sense, I guess, since she was now standing in front of God. It was like she had decided to wear her fanciest Easter dress to meet Him in person.

Lavish Grace. She always laughed at her name. She had been Lavish Spears before she married my grandpa. But when Lavish Spears married Tom Grace, she became Lavish Grace, and that's when the whole journey I want to tell you about began—my grandmother, her life, and why she meant so much to me. I am her firstborn grandson. Christopher James Grace. That's me. Most folks call me Chris, but I prefer Christopher. That just sounds better.

Anyway, I swallowed kind of hard. I closed my eyes. And I stuck out my hand. I touched her. First, I put my hand on her arm, on top of the sleeve of that Easter dress. That was safer than touching her skin. I rubbed that dress for a second or two. It was soft to touch, just like I remembered it.

But then, when she didn't jump or move or sit up, I moved my hand down her arm. The skin was still soft, but her arm was real hard and cold. I think they had makeup on her skin too, because I got a bunch of powder stuff on my hands. I had to go to the bathroom to wash that off. I didn't want anybody to find out I had touched my dead grandmother. That would be gross.

For a minute or two, I just stood there. And I rubbed her arm. Then I touched her face. It was really stiff. But it felt good to touch her even if her face was cold.

It was still her. My grandmother. And touching her made me remember.

First, I remembered Grandma Lavish telling me about touching Father Cascia's dead body on the boat deck after he saved her from drowning. I wondered if his skin had felt like Grandma Lavish's did now.

Then I remembered a bunch of other stuff. All kinds of things about Grandma Lavish. Cooking and baking with her. How special Christmas was at her house. But especially the bracelet. I'll tell you about that in a minute, if you can hang on.

It was nice, being there with her all by myself. I missed her. Tears started running down my face, so I looked around for a box of Kleenex. But touching her for a moment brought her back. Sort of. I mean, I knew she was dead and all that, but it felt good to be there with her and to see her in that pretty dress.

She didn't move, thank goodness. There was a part of me that was scared I might poke Grandma Lavish and she would sit up right there in Forrest Funeral Home and stare me in the eye and ask, "What do you think you are doing, Christopher?" But she didn't.

Nothing happened. So I walked back down the hall to find my parents, feeling a little bigger than I had just a few minutes before. She might be dead, but her skin was still skin. And I had touched it. All by myself. And I was the only one who knew about it.

I went back down to the office and found my parents. By then, all of our family was showing up, and Mr. Forrest was telling everybody what to do. He was trying to get us all together for a picture before we went to see Grandma Lavish. It was like he was the crossing guard at my school, pointing everybody in the right direction. I don't think anybody even noticed that I had been gone. And I sure didn't tell them that I had touched her. That was just gonna be our little secret. Me and Grandma Lavish. I told you she was special.

There were about fifty of us, counting all my cousins and everybody. We walked down the hall, and went into the room where Grandma Lavish was. We stood around the casket. Mom made us all hold hands. My dad said a prayer. So did the priest.

Then everybody took turns walking up and looking into the casket at Grandma Lavish, staring at her in that pretty dress she'd always said she got on sale at Macy's that time she went to New York. I led my brother, Michael, by the hand, and I touched her again. Michael was too scared to do it. He's chicken like that. But I'm not. I winked at her like it was my first time. I think I saw her smile back at me for a second, but Dad says I'm crazy.

Anyway, everybody in my whole family stood around Grandma Lavish for a few minutes. I was the only grandchild with enough guts to touch her. And then people began to fill the room. People from all over town, and even some from out of state, came to see Grandma Lavish and talk to my family. Some folks call that a visitation. We call it a wake.

We had planned to stand there and visit with people for two hours. That's what the sign said:

But the people kept coming. And coming. They lined up down the hallway and all the way out the back door of Forrest Funeral Home, onto the sidewalk and into the parking lot. I thought there were two million people there, but Dad said it was just five hundred or something like that.

People laughed. They told stories. They cried. I remember that too. Nearly all of them wanted to talk to my grandfather, Tom Grace. He was seventy-three then, a couple of years older than Grandma Lavish, and he did not feel very good either. Not just because Grandma Lavish, his wife of more than fifty years, had died. Anyone would feel bad if that happened. But Grandpa had cancer too, just like the stuff that had killed Grandma Lavish. And it made him tired most of the time.

Grandpa stood there, and he took it like a man. That's what my dad said. "Christopher, your grandpa greeted everybody and stood there for hours. He really took it like a man."

Grandpa stood there for four full hours. Never sat down once. He wanted to honor Grandma Lavish and all those millions of people and greet each one squarely in the eye, and let them share all of their stories about her. Greeting these people meant something to Grandpa. To me, it just felt like watching the news on TV, where people just talk and talk about stuff nobody cares about. Or a really long movie that never ends. All these people, all this noise and talking. Having to wear a tie and stand up and talk with grown-ups. I didn't like that either. This was my first wake and my first funeral home. The only good news was Grandma Lavish was my very first dead body to touch. Other than that, this stank.

Grandpa stood in that one spot while my dad walked around the room. Dad smiled and chitchatted with all the guests. It seemed like he knew most of them even though I had no idea who all these people were. Dad seemed so at ease as he listened to the visitors talk about his mother, my Grandma Lavish. He soaked in their stories like a dry sponge under a faucet when you're getting ready to wash the car.

Dad listened as an older man got right in his face and yelled. Like Dad was as hard of hearing as the old man speaking or something.

"Hello, you're old and can't hear!" I wanted to say. "Dad can hear you just fine."

Everyone could hear that man tell Dad how Grandma Lavish had paid for his truck. The megaphone-mouthed man said that he and his wife had gotten themselves stretched too thin years ago with two kids and a pregnancy and no way to pay for the birth of their child. Somehow, Grandma Lavish had quietly gone to the bank and paid off the note on the family's truck and gently told the man to use the money he would have spent on the truck to pay for the birth of his new baby.

A young woman with two small children came over to Dad too. She was having a hard time, juggling her two little kids and all. But you could tell she was determined to let my father know how Grandma Lavish had made it possible for her to attend St. Catherine's School even though her parents could never have paid for Catholic school for her. She was so proud of her education. She even wanted to share the school's special pledge aloud for Dad to hear so she could prove that she really had been paying attention all those years she had been on scholarship thanks to my Grandma Lavish and everything.

A third woman came up with tears in her eyes. She said her name was Sarah Heaton. She talked about the day she had scooped up her children and run away in the car with nothing but the clothes they were wearing. Dad said Mr. Heaton had had a bad habit of letting his fist run into his wife's face, especially when he drank too much. I guess that happened a lot. Finally she found the courage to leave. When she did, she had no plan. She just wanted to keep her children safe from a drunk man so scary that she did not see how they could survive. She drove like crazy to St. Catherine's Church, knowing somehow that someone there would find a way to help.

Grandma Lavish happened to be in the parking lot that day. She was always at the church for one thing or another. Grandpa called her the church lady. Anyway, this young mom collapsed in tears in front of her. Grandma Lavish listened to the mother's crying, made a phone call to a safe house, and took the whole family there. She even helped them move into a small house in a new town when the mother found a job there. Grandma Lavish paid their rent for two years. When Mrs. Heaton heard about Grandma Lavish's death, she knew she had to drive back to Lake Bobola just to tell all the family thanks.

I mean, there were all kinds of people, and every one of them had a story of some kind to tell us. And every few minutes or so, Dad would walk over and hand Grandpa a cup of cool water. He knew that it was hard for Grandpa to stand there and greet every person and listen to their grateful story or kind words about Grandma Lavish. But that was Dad, taking care of his sad father even while entertaining two million other people in a small room for four hours. He made me proud.

The wake was supposed to end at seven o'clock, but the people just kept coming and coming. No one wanted to turn them away. There were just too many people. Father Fisher arrived around seven to do all the stuff priests do at wakes, but he had to wait until eight thirty or so before he began leading us all in praying the rosary. The crowd started to go away a bit then. But it was really cool. Father Fisher helped us remember Grandma Lavish and give thanks to God for her life. He listened to some of our stories. He even wrote down a few notes so that he could use those stories at the funeral Mass.

We were there for more than four hours. Can you believe it? Jillions of people, Father Fisher, Dad, Grandpa, and me. For as long as I am alive, I will remember that day. It was the first time I touched a dead body. But I also learned something really big about Grandma Lavish and her bracelet.

I'll get to that in a minute.

3 : THE FUNERAL

The wake was on Friday. Father Fisher celebrated the funeral Mass the next day, on Saturday afternoon. Our little church, St. Catherine of Siena, has room for four hundred people or so, but on that day, no one could even count how many people came to Mass to remember my grandmother. The church was full. So was the parish hall, where they set up a little television to show what was happening in the church. So were the hallways and the front porch and nearly any other space anywhere on the whole property. If there were two million people at Grandma's wake, at least twice that many showed up for her funeral. My dad says it was probably more like a thousand, but he didn't actually count them.

I've gotta be honest, it was a weird day—all these people arriving together to talk about my grandmother, who wasn't even there to hear it. I missed her. I missed how she filled every room as soon as she walked in. I'm not sure how she did that, but everybody knew she did. When Grandma Lavish was around, everybody just felt better. She had a way of doing that. She made you feel like you were better than you really were. Then it dawned on me that that warm feeling of just her being there would never happen again.

So there I was, ten years old, weaving in and out of a bunch of people I didn't know. Father Fisher was standing in front of the crowd and telling them that this was the hardest and easiest funeral Mass he had ever celebrated. Hardest because Grandma had meant so much to him. Easy because she was so special and he knew that her resurrection dress was the perfect one for her to be wearing as she got ready to meet the Lord.

Plus, seeing all my cousins and family dressed up like it was Easter. To me, as a ten-year-old, it was just plain weird. I really wanted Grandma Lavish to be there. After all, this was really about her, and it didn't seem right that she wasn't there to be a part of it.

Father Fisher had been the priest at St. Catherine's ever since before I was born, so he knew all about Grandma Lavish. He loved her just like all of us did. When he talked about her, he meant it. You could see it in his face. But I had never seen him like this before. He was nervous. He stopped every few minutes to wipe the tears off his face. I mean, he was a mess. Kind of reminded me of Mrs. Rushin, my English teacher, who cries every time she reads us a poem. But nothing was going to stop Father Fisher from saying what he wanted to say at the funeral Mass for Mrs. Lavish Grace.

He fumbled around. Everybody kept listening because he loved my grandmother a bunch. He shared some stories about her. Father Fisher loved when Grandma Lavish baked him cakes and left them on his desk at the church. And he always knew that when someone needed help, he could call

Grandma Lavish because she would respond. When he said that, I heard a few people mumble amen.

Some of this stuff he said was stuff I had never heard before. Like when he compared Grandma Lavish to the woman who had anointed Jesus's feet with oil and her hair. When Father Fisher mentioned her, he looked at me and my cousins and told us how lucky we were to be related to her. But we already knew that.

As Father Fisher finished the Mass, the pallbearers lifted Grandma Lavish's big old casket and carried it out the door. Those eight men walked with puffed-out chests. Dad said it was because they knew that bunches of people wanted to carry Grandma Lavish but only they had received the honor of marching with her on her last journey on this earth.

The men staggered through the parking lot. I thought they were gonna fall down a couple of times. It was hot, and that casket was heavy. They refused to use the Forrest Funeral Home cart that those men in black suits kept pushing beside the casket just in case the men ran out of steam and couldn't make it any farther. The guys moved together like soldiers marching from the church, through the parking lot, all the way to the parish cemetery next door. That place was spooky. It had jillions of old graves dating all the way back to the 1800s. That's when our parish was settled and established. I learned that at school.

Lake Bobola has been around a long time. It's not a town like a lot of those beach places in Florida. Some Spanish people settled here a long time ago, like before the Civil War. Don't ask me how they lived here without air-conditioning. I have no idea, but they did build a pretty town. We even have an old fort they built to keep the town safe.

This place really was Grandma Lavish's home; my grandmother had loved Lake Bobola, and she had loved her parish. Nothing would have made her happier than to know she would be laid to rest with so many people helping in her favorite place.

When we got to the graveside, the pallbearers laid her casket on the metal thing the men in black suits would use to lower her into the ground. The coffin just sat there, and Father Fisher said the final words of our send-off to my grandmother.

He spoke, and the people prayed. I opened my eyes and looked around. I just knew this moment was special. This was it. My last chance with Grandma Lavish. It hurt so much to know I wouldn't ever see her face again smiling at me and laughing.

I looked at all the people. The little tent by the grave was full. People stood all around it. Nobody cared about the nasty Florida summer heat or how sweaty they were getting. We all just wanted to be nearby when Lavish Grace got put into her final place of rest. Everybody just knew. This was it. The end.

I had never seen so many people before in my life. Where did they all come from? Why were they still hanging around? Did Grandma really know all these folks? I just couldn't believe that. Folks in Lake Bobola liked to show up for funerals, but this was crazy. I mean, people were everywhere, and I had no idea who most of them were.

When Father Fisher finished with all his words, he looked at Grandpa, and asked, "Tom, would you like to say anything else before we take this final step with Lavish?" You had to know my grandfather to get what he did next. He didn't care how many people were there or what everybody expected him to do. Grandpa was a strong man, and he just blurted out to Father Fisher, "Open her casket one more time. I want to say good-bye one last time."

Some people laughed, thinking Grandpa was joking about reopening the casket. Others teared up. They knew we were witnessing something special between a man and his wife.

Father Fisher knew Grandpa, so he told the men in the black suits to open the casket one final time. As they did, Grandpa leaned over and kissed Grandma Lavish on the cheek, and whispered, "I love you, Lavish. I always have. Good-bye. I'll see you on the other side of the river. Good-bye."

Grandpa rubbed Grandma Lavish's arm, in the exact same place I had touched her in the funeral home. And then he turned away and began to walk off.

Father Fisher sprinkled dirt over the open grave and reminded us that we are all made of dust and to dust we shall return. Or something like that. Dad said it was like the words they say on Ash Wednesday when they rub all that stuff on your head.

And that was it. It was over.

Lots of folks came up to Grandpa one last time to show their love before they left the cemetery. All of our family just stood around the grave site, watching as the men shoveled in dirt to fill up Grandma Lavish's grave. That was just what she had wanted. She wanted everybody to see the dirt being put on top of her grave like that. In fact, she had written down directions for everything about her burial: no machines, no backhoes, only real men and real shovels, and she wanted it done while we all stood there and watched. Dad said that was how it oughta be. He said that Grandma Lavish wanted everybody at her funeral, and anyone else who was watching, to know that death comes to us all. "You prepare for death; you don't fear it," she wrote down in the directions. This was her way of teaching us one more time, even though she was dead.

Finally, all those people left. Then my father stepped up next to Grandpa and took him by the hand. "It was a good day. Mom would have been proud. Let's go home."

Grandpa just nodded and started to walk back toward the church.

As we walked slowly back out of the cemetery, Dad was on one side of Grandpa and I was on the other. I looked up at this old man, and I asked him, "Grandpa, did you see how many people came? It was amazing."

Grandpa looked down at me. "It was because she was so generous."

"What do you mean?" I replied.

Then he just said, "Come see me tonight." Grandpa wiped a tear off his cheek and got in the car to go home.

4: THE BRACELET

You have to grow up in Florida to understand hot. Grandpa loved to say, "Hell hath no fury like the Florida sun." Not sure where he got that, but it was true.

That's why I liked to ride my bike at night, especially in the summer. Riding at night meant the heat wouldn't suck the life out of you. So, when Grandpa said, "Come see me tonight," I smiled because that meant I would get to ride to his house in the dark. And after a day like we'd had at Grandma Lavish's funeral, I really wanted just to sit with my grandfather and be. Just be.

After supper, I told Mom my plan to ride down to Grandpa's house for a while to check on him. The ride didn't take long; Grandpa lived just a few blocks away. The street had live oaks on both sides for most of the way. I had ridden that road a thousand times, I think. Seeing the moon through those live oaks felt almost like Halloween every single time. And the Spanish moss hanging off the branches made it feel even more spooky at night.

I rode up into Grandpa's front yard, jumped off my bike, and ran into the house. He sat in his familiar brown recliner. It was kind of worn out from many years of watching

Braves baseball games. Next to the chair, on the floor, sat the little Maxwell House coffee can that Grandpa used for his chewing tobacco spit. He loved that stuff. Not me—I tried it once and puked for two days.

One time, in art class in second grade, the teacher asked me to draw something special. So I drew a picture of Grandpa in that big old brown chair. He was a small man, and that chair made him look like a baseball in a big catcher's mitt.

He smiled when he saw me. "Christopher, where you been? Have a seat."

I sat on the floor on the rug in the middle of the room, right between Grandpa's chair and the television. I wanted all of his attention tonight—no distractions from baseball games or weather reports on the TV. I crossed my legs and stared at him just like we looked at the librarian at school when she would read us stories. Grandpa's eyes just looked so sad, and the creases on his face looked deeper than they did before.

Without Grandma Lavish in the house, the place felt too big, too quiet, and too empty to me. All you noticed was the big space and the big silence. It was weird.

"What'd you think about the funeral, Christopher?" Grandpa asked me.

"It was weird," I said.

"Weird?"

"Yes, weird. All those people, with all of them wanting to tell a story about Grandma Lavish. Weird. They all seemed to care about her so much, but I didn't even know who any of them were."

"People loved your grandmother very much," Grandpa replied.

I looked around the room and saw all the photos on the wall: pictures of our family in all kinds of places; Christmas at Grandma Lavish's house; family reunion at the lake; one shot from my all-star baseball game. The pictures just stared back at me.

It all came back to the same thing: Grandma Lavish was gone.

"Grandpa, why do you think no one wanted to leave the cemetery? Why wouldn't they go home?"

Grandpa took a deep breath.

"Your grandmother was special, Christopher. She was a giver. And people loved her for that. I don't think she ever really knew how many people she had touched. She never realized how much people loved her. She just loved to give. And today you saw the results. Those people were there out of love."

Grandpa looked at the rubber bracelet I was wearing.

"I miss her, Grandpa," I said.

Then he looked at me. I think he was hurting even more than I was. He asked me if he could hold my bracelet. So I handed it to him. He wove it in and out through his fingers and stared at it as he moved it across the palm of his hand.

He slowly began to speak. "Her bracelet. The one she always wore. That's why so many people showed up at the wake and the funeral. Because of her bracelet, Christopher."

Of course, I knew the bracelet. Grandma Lavish not only wore it all the time; she used it to teach me about her life more times than I can remember.

When I would spend the night at their house, we liked to stay up late watching a movie. Lots of times, she would walk me through the four letters printed on the bracelet: L-E-G-S. When we went camping at the lake for two weeks every summer around the Fourth of July, Grandma Lavish would tell me about LEGS as we sat by the fire and made snacks with marshmallows and chocolate. With her, everything always seemed to come back to LEGS. And those four letters stood out—black letters on a bright orange rubber bracelet.

I knew exactly what those letters stood for. I even remembered the first time I noticed Grandma Lavish's LEGS bracelet. Grandpa and Grandma Lavish had come over to our house to take care of me while my parents went out one night. Michael had just been born, and Mom and Dad wanted a little peace and quiet, they said. Grandma Lavish was sitting on the floor playing Go Fish with me while Grandpa rocked Michael back and forth in the little cradle in the den. Grandma Lavish dealt the cards, and I looked down and saw it for the very first time. That one and only LEGS bracelet.

L: Love all you can
E: Earn all you can
G: Give all you can
S: Save all you can

As I sat there in the middle of the den with Grandpa and remembered all the times Grandma Lavish had talked to me about LEGS, a smile broke out on my face. In my mind I could picture how Grandma Lavish, even after I was reading grown-up books, would point to each letter on that bracelet as if she were teaching me the alphabet again for the very first time.

"*L*, Christopher. That *L* stands for 'Love all you can.'"

I don't know why she did that. It was like she didn't remember the zillion times she had told me that before. Maybe she thought it was funny to always say that same phrase, just to pick at me like I was still four years old or something. One thing is for sure: She wanted me to remember those simple letters. She always said the very same thing. Every single time.

"*E*, Christopher," as she pointed to the letter on her bracelet. "That *E* stands for 'Earn all you can.'"

When I remembered her doing that and chuckled, it must have startled Grandpa. I think he was lost in his own pleasant thoughts and memories, just rubbing that little bracelet. He looked up and said, "Come over here, Christopher."

I stood up and moved toward Grandpa and the overstuffed chair. He reached out and gave me a big hug. I hated those hugs. I always squirmed when anybody tried to give me one, but this time Grandpa wouldn't let go until he was ready.

Then he said, "Christopher, let me keep the bracelet tonight. I just like to hold it. Come back tomorrow if you can.

When you do, I'll tell you where that bracelet came from. Grandma Lavish never told you that. And if you're gonna wear this bracelet, you need to know the whole story."

5: THE MEMORIES

All the way home from Grandpa's, I thought about Grandma Lavish. I didn't sleep much that night either. I wanted to hear about where her bracelet had come from. And memories of special things just kept popping into my brain. Dad said that's what you do when somebody special dies. And this was the first time I had ever really known anybody who died.

I missed her, especially the smell of her baking. Does that sound weird? You didn't know her, but nobody could beat Grandma Lavish when it came to the kitchen. When you walked into her house, you walked into sweet smells better than any bakery you've ever been to. And I know. I go in the bakery every time I ride my bike downtown looking for baseball cards. Cupcakes, pies, and even bread— Grandma Lavish loved to bake. And nobody could do it like she could.

Grandma Lavish had her own special way of creating the perfect strawberry cake. You'd love it. It was my favorite; she made it for me every birthday. A recipe "never seen by human eyes since the beginning of time," she would tell me. And a recipe taught on the job in the kitchen so you could eyeball her as she sprinkled those fresh strawberries right into the batter and the icing. Man, that was some good stuff.

Grandma Lavish would never tell anybody the recipe, but she would walk you through the steps of making that batter, mixing it just so, and then carefully placing it in the pans for baking. Anybody who asked could learn it from her. Just not in writing. I don't think she even had it in writing. Maybe she just carried it around in her head. She said she was blessed to be the one lady on the planet who knew the secret Spears family strawberry cake recipe. Anyway, that was my grandmother. She loved to bake, and I loved to eat.

I missed how it felt with her in the house. Everything just felt so warm when she was around. I felt special as the oldest grandchild. I was the first grandson, and it was like I was the only one. There was no secret recipe for how Grandma Lavish accomplished that; it just seemed to happen naturally. She looked you in the eye; she listened to every word you said; she really paid attention to you—she even kept a notebook filled up with dates and important things she wanted to remember about you.

Grandma Lavish knew me. I mean, she really knew me, in that deep down way where I believed she knew what I was going to do before I even thought about doing it. That made me feel like the most important person on the planet. And around Grandma Lavish, I was.

Anyway, when I was lying in bed that night after her funeral, it hit me like a ton of bricks: She was gone. Really gone.

She told me once that becoming a grandmother was the moment she had been waiting for her entire life. The moment she would go from being a wife and mother into what she called "the sacred role of grandmother." She knew exactly what she would do when she got to be a grandmother. She would pay back every bit of love she had gotten from her own Granny by pouring that same love into the lives of her grandchildren.

And that special moment became the story I loved to hear the most, probably because it was all about my own birth as the very first grandchild in the Grace family. Who doesn't like to hear about when they were born?

When Mom and Dad headed to the hospital around midnight on December 28, 1988, they drove like crazy through Lake Bobola to the labor and delivery entrance at Tanner Medical Center just like they had practiced over and over.

Dad called his parents, Tom and Lavish. You already know about them. So they were also speeding through the night to see me get born. Dad said missiles and rockets could have been headed toward Florida that night, but nothing was gonna stop Mrs. Lavish Grace from being there when her first grandchild showed up.

Grandma Lavish and Grandpa sat out in the waiting room. Every once in a while Dad would give them an update on how Mom and the delivery were coming along. Grandma Lavish paced the floor. Grandpa just sat and read *Sports Illustrated.* Of course, he had to step outside the hospital to spit out the tobacco juice that usually landed in the Maxwell House can by his chair at home. Grandma Lavish walked around with her rosary beads in hand, quietly praying and asking for the help of the Virgin Mary (and Mary's very own newborn baby, Jesus).

In the middle of all that, at 6:27 a.m. on December 28, I was born. Christopher James Grace. The first child of Gary and Jacqueline Grace. More important, the very first grandchild of Tom and Lavish Grace.

At 6:32, Dad stepped out into the lobby to share the news with my grandparents. Grandma Lavish jumped at the door and ran into the room to be near my mom to see the first sight of the new child. The nurses had just placed me in the arms of my mom, who always says she was tired but thrilled after getting me safely into the world. We were resting in her bed. Grandma Lavish didn't even stop to think. She just scooped me up, her newborn grandson. Grandpa said she acted like a mama eagle, swooping down to rescue her offspring from danger. Grandma Lavish lifted me into her arms and stared into my eyes. For what seemed like hours, or so everyone tells me, Grandma Lavish lost herself in the deep blue eyes of her first grandchild, little Christopher Grace, also known as me.

I loved to hear that story again and again. Anytime I could get a family member to share it, the story of my birth and my first face-to-face meeting with Grandma Lavish made me feel loved. And special.

Anyway, you get the deal. Trying to go to sleep after Grandma Lavish's funeral just was not easy for me. The images kept popping into my brain like little pieces of pop-corn in the cooker at the movie theater. I smiled because I loved my grandmother more than meat loves salt. I really wanted to be around her from the moment I first remembered meeting her. Now you know why. Just for the warmth. The love. To stand near her in the kitchen, to play cards after dinner, to walk through her garden and talk, or simply to snuggle up on the couch and watch a movie. There just was no place like being in the same place as Grandma Lavish.

And I loved to hear her stories. I told those stories to myself over and over that night after her funeral. Seeing her face in my mind helped me calm down and finally go to sleep. I was hoping that somehow she would show up in my dreams that night just so I could touch her again.

6: THE MOMENT

The next morning, I got up with only one thing on my mind: I wanted to see Grandpa. I wanted to check on him, but mainly I wanted to hear where Grandma Lavish's bracelet had come from. He had promised to tell me.

So I jumped on my bike and headed to Grandpa's house. It still felt a little weird to me that Grandma Lavish wouldn't be there. It just didn't seem right.

As soon as I walked in, Grandpa looked at me from his chair and said, "You want some lunch?"

"But it's only ten thirty, Grandpa," I said back.

"Yeah. I eat when I get hungry, and I'm hungry. So let's fix a sandwich, Christopher."

He got up and we went into the kitchen. It was the first time I had been in Grandma Lavish's kitchen since she died. It still smelled like her. Man, I missed her.

Grandpa pulled out some bread and some lunch meat. We each made a sandwich just like we wanted. I made a turkey sandwich with lettuce and mayo. No tomatoes for me. I hate those things. Grandpa got all the meat in the refrigerator and put some Tabasco sauce on top. Don't ask me why he sprinkled hot sauce on sandwiches. Nobody knew why he did that. I always figured it had something to do with the tobacco juice killing his taste buds.

We sat down at the kitchen table, in the same chairs we always sat in. Except this time, Grandma Lavish's chair, nearest the stove, sat empty.

Grandpa spoke first.

"You see where she got the idea for the bracelet, Christopher? From Father Cascia. That image of a 'Love' bracelet always stayed in her memory.

"She started putting the pieces together for herself. Your Grandma Lavish always loved going to church. Even when she was a little girl. After she nearly drowned, barely a day went by that your grandmother did not at least stop in for a few minutes to pray. She would go to Mass if the schedule hit just right, but it was important to her at least to stop in and pray and think about God. She was just six years old. Amazing to me. The thought would never have occurred to me. I'd rather have been anywhere than in a church. Six years old?! But I guess almost dying does that to you.

"Somehow, the Church felt like home to Grandma Lavish. Anytime we were near one, she felt this pull. She said it was like how gravity pulls a rock down to earth when you drop it. She felt pulled into the Church. Maybe she felt grateful to Father Cascia for saving her life. Or maybe she just really loved God with all her heart. And she knew Jesus was present in the Church and wanted to say hello.

"Growing up, your Grandma Lavish would sit in that chapel over there at St. Catherine's by herself. She told me what she loved to do most was stare at the crucifix. With

Jesus hanging there, the crown on His head, and the little drops of blood painted on His hands and feet and face.

"She developed that habit early on. First grade, I think. And it just stuck, I guess. For years before I ever even knew her, your grandmother was stopping by that prayer chapel nearly every day leading all the way up to high school.

"While we were dating, there were two years there when she was still back here in Lake Bobola while I was in Atlanta at college at Georgia Tech. I had tried to go into the Army because of the big war, but I failed the physical and I went off to college instead. One of those years, when I came home from school for break, she shared with me something that had happened in that prayer chapel.

"'Tommy,' she said. She loved to call me Tommy because she knew I hated it. I made everybody else call me Tom.

"'Tommy, I was on my way to pray in the chapel two weeks ago. It was raining outside, so I sat in the car after I parked at the church and gathered my things and my umbrella before I got out in that mess.

"'When I stepped out of the car, some lady I had never seen walked up beside me. She didn't have an umbrella. I guess she wanted to sneak under with me, so I let her. Then she started telling me about this news story that day that I had not heard about.

"'Up in Jacksonville, the manager of an apartment complex was walking around the buildings last week when he heard a weird noise coming out of one of the vacant apartments. Sounded like a scratching of some sort. He thought it was a mouse or a squirrel inside the wall or something, so he made a mental note to stop in the next day and see what he needed to do to keep that apartment ready for rental. Well, the next day came, and he heard that same noise with a mild whimpering sound too, but he was really busy and didn't have time to check on that vacant apartment, so he wrote down on his to-do list to be sure and check in on that apartment the next day.

"'Finally, on that third day, the manager opened the vacant apartment where he was hearing that scratching and whimpering. He figured he'd find a cat or some animal that had gotten in through a window or something. But he didn't see anything. He walked through the kitchen and the eating areas of the apartment and into the den. Nothing. Walked down the hall and stuck his head in the first two bedrooms and the bathroom. Still nothing.

"'Eventually, he got to the third bedroom in that empty apartment. Still, he didn't see anything until he opened the closet door in the bedroom. On the floor in front of him was a little seven-year-old boy, totally naked, and covered in cockroaches and his hand stuck down into a jar of peanut butter. Nothing else in the closet or the whole apartment. This little boy had been there for days, all by himself. His family, if you can call them that, had just left him. Nobody knows for sure but they think the grown-ups moved away and just left this little boy behind to fend for himself.

"'Can you believe that, Tommy? A mother would actually just abandon her little son. For what? For drug money or something? What in the world is the matter with that lady?

"'Well, the woman walking beside me under the umbrella went on into the church building and headed down the hall. I turned the other way and went into the little prayer chapel.

"'I was the only one in there. Since it was raining outside, it was nice and peaceful inside. Completely quiet in the chapel except for the little pitter-pat on the roof from the raindrops. And I focused on the crucifix again like I usually do. I pictured that little boy sitting in the closet by himself. And just kept lifting my heart up to that cross to Jesus and asking for His help. For the little boy. For kids who get treated like used cigarette butts and need love. And for me. Just wanting Him to show me some way I could make that kid's life a little better.

"'I stared at the crucifix for a while. Meditated, I guess you'd call it. And then I would close my eyes and Father Cascia and that day at the lake began to come to my mind. I'd open my eyes and gaze again at the crucifix, close my eyes and Father Cascia would come back to my mind. For fifteen, maybe twenty minutes. Back and forth. Back and forth between Jesus and Father Cascia.

"'This may not make much sense, because it's really hard to explain something like this. But for a minute or two in the middle of that, it was like I was the only person on the planet. Everything else in my mind just shut out. A misty fog came and settled onto the prayer chapel all around me. It was just me, the crucifix, and the image of Father Cascia in the middle of all this mist. And I had this overwhelming sense of being surrounded by God, by the Holy Spirit.'

"She kept going. 'I love to pray each day in that chapel, and on some days I feel more connected to God than on others. But never have I experienced this, ever. It was like God was leading me into a place in Him and in myself that had not been touched before. It was like Father Cascia was standing right there next to Jesus on the crucifix. And somehow that was connected to my heart breaking for that little seven-year-old boy. I know this doesn't make sense but I have to tell you. Nobody else would even begin to understand. They'd think I was crazy.

"'For a moment—and I have no idea how long it really was—it felt completely out of time and space to me. I didn't care about anything else; I noticed nothing else. I was totally wrapped into the presence of God, Jesus suffering on that crucifix, and the presence of Father Cascia.

"'And then I looked, and Father Cascia was placing his hand on Jesus's heart. I couldn't see his face. And I couldn't hear a thing. But time stood still. And I was witness to an act of pure devotion. Father Cascia with his hand on the heart of Jesus hanging on that crucifix.

"'And it began to make sense to me. The cross is love. Jesus comes to us out of love. Being willing to suffer, even willing to die, because of love. My words really cannot capture what was taking place down deep inside me. A love so full that I cannot even describe it. So deep, so warm, so pure. It was like my heart was about to burst.

"'I kept meditating and realized that in a way that is exactly what happens every time I receive the Eucharist. It really is the body and blood of Jesus. He is coming straight to me. Straight into me, really. He comes to me in the Eucharist and gives Himself to me. That is love. And now every single time I receive the body and blood, my heart just nearly explodes. Because of the incredible love.

"'And in that vision, or whatever you want to call it, Father Cascia became a part of all that. I remembered the bracelet. And I remembered his sacrifice to save me from drowning. Father Cascia gave his life for a tiny child, me. And then I thought about all the little sacrifices he made along the way just to be a priest. The education. Not being able to marry or have kids. Having little or no money. Sharing his time and his life with the people of the community rather than with a family of his own. Giving himself away kind of like Jesus on the cross. In little bits at a time.

"'And I just knew. Way deep down in a peaceful way. It all made sense. Love. The cross. Jesus. The body and the blood. Father Cascia. Jessica and me at the lake. The little boy by himself in the closet at that apartment. And Father Cascia's bracelet. Love.

"'Do you see it, Tommy? Does that make sense? All the parts fit together. God is not only a giver; He is the Supreme Giver. He not only gives life; He gives us Himself. And that was Father Cascia. He did the exact same thing.

"'Tommy, I need to tell you that I have made a decision.'"

Grandpa stopped for a second. He knew he had me in the palm of his hand. And he wanted me to wait for a second before he finished. Then he said, "Christopher, at that moment, I thought I was gonna lose the love of my life. I would have bet your whole baseball card collection that she was gonna tell me that she was breaking up with me to go become a nun."

I looked at Grandpa. My eyes were about to pop out of my forehead. I leaned my ears toward him at the table as if somehow I could get to the answer sooner.

"But then your grandmother said, 'Tommy, I don't want to live halfway. I don't want to be halfhearted. I want to love and I want no one ever to doubt that I love them. Not just you. You know that I love you. But I mean, I want to love completely. That's what Jesus said is the main thing. All the way. Love God. Love people. Love little children who need help and basic love. Why do something only halfway? Do you want to meet Saint Peter and have him ask you why you lived life at half speed? Not me!'"

Grandpa paused again. I think he was waiting for me to say something. Or maybe he was just all caught up in this special memory from a long time ago. But this whole story was weird to me. It was strange to me to think about Grandma Lavish taking classes at the little college in Lake Bobola, not even married to Grandpa then. How could Grandma Lavish be all young like that? I didn't know what to say.

Grandpa just looked so sad. He sat there at the table for a minute, maybe two. His eyes teared up, and he picked up a napkin to wipe them.

"*Love all you can.* God is love. Once your grandmother discovered that in that prayer chapel, Christopher, she never looked back. I have got more to tell you, but that was the moment. She never questioned it again. All her prayer time for all those years led her to that one special moment. And from that point forward, she had made the decision: She was going to love all she could.

"I didn't really know what that meant at the time. But, boy, it didn't take her long to show me."

Grandpa stopped talking.

"Keep going, Grandpa. I want to hear everything you can tell me about the bracelet. Keep going. Please. You said I needed to know the whole story."

But he just stood up and said, "I'm going to bed."

7 : THE TALENTS

It seemed like forever before I got to spend time alone with Grandpa again. Everyone was just so busy with stuff. I never knew you had to do so many things when somebody dies.

Of course, I saw Grandpa every day. Just never alone. That's because he was spending lots of time talking to my dad about things that didn't make any sense to me. Wills. Social Security. Flowers. Stuff like that.

Everybody was writing thank-you notes to all the people who had done such nice things for our family when Grandma Lavish died. I helped with the notes for the food. That was easy. Our kitchen was piled high with plates and pans that had been full of good food people had brought over to our house. I'm not sure why everybody brought food, but I was glad they did. Tuna casserole. Hash browns with cheese. Chocolate cake with fudge icing. I was eating like a king. So the least I could do was help write a few of the thank-you notes for the feast.

Saturday rolled around, and I was worried Grandpa wouldn't want to talk about Grandma Lavish and the bracelet anymore. So I just rode my bike down to his house, jumped up the front porch steps, and went in. Of course, I found him in the usual place. Recliner. Chewing tobacco in his mouth. But the television was off. Grandpa was sitting there all quiet and stuff. By himself, just thinking, I guess.

His eyes lit up when I walked in.

"How you doing, kid? Glad you're here."

"Good morning, Grandpa. You not watching TV?

"Not today, Christopher. Maybe later when the game comes on. Just sitting here thinking about your Grandma Lavish."

I missed her too.

"Grandpa, can I have the bracelet back now? And what happened after Grandma Lavish made that decision you told me about, to love all she could? You said you were gonna tell me how she got that bracelet. And you haven't said another word since."

"I figured you'd come back and want to hear more. And now's as good a time as any to share it with you. Sit down, son.

"I told you the other day how your grandmother loved to pray. How she carved out ten or fifteen minutes each day to sit with the Lord and listen. Sometimes she would sit in that prayer chapel at church for an hour, but no matter what, she always had at least some time each day just to be with God.

"Well, a lot of her days, she would read the Bible. That was part of her prayer time. Read one of the psalms. Or maybe a teaching from Jesus. She'd sit and meditate on that passage of the Bible. She liked to listen for what God might say to her when she focused like that.

"I guess it was a year or so after that day she told me about her vision in the chapel. Maybe a little more. I was still a student at Tech, but we were talking about getting married as soon as I graduated.

"Anyway, I was home for the summer. And I went with her to the prayer chapel one day. That summer, I was working at the mill sweeping floors to earn some money for school. Grandma Lavish and I would meet most days right after I got off work. We liked to eat dinner together, just the two of us. That way we could talk about what had happened during our days. Her job was sitting with a neighbor, an old woman who needed company during the day. So the family paid Lavish to sit with her, read some books and the mail to her, keep her company, do a little cleaning, that kind of thing.

"Well, evidently, that day the old woman slept most of the time. So your grandmother spent her whole day reading the Bible."

Grandpa paused and chuckled.

"What's so funny, Grandpa?" I asked.

He answered, "Nothing, really. I was just thinking about me sweeping floors all day and there your grandmother was getting paid to read the Bible. One of her favorite things to do. And she was getting paid to do it while that old woman slept. Meanwhile, I was working my fanny off in the Florida heat inside a mill. Grandma Lavish always seemed to get off easy that way. She was just lucky, I guess.

"So we met after work that day. Walked down to the river and sat down to eat on the grass. Grandma Lavish loved to have a picnic. Not me. I hate eating outside. Always have. Bugs and all that crap. Plus who wants to eat in the heat outside when you've been sweeping floors all day in a hot mill? But she loved to eat outside, and I loved her, so we ate outside. That's how love works, Christopher. You'd better get used to it.

"While we were eating our sandwiches, she told me about her day. She had been reading a parable of Jesus, the parable of the talents. You ever heard of that one, Christopher?"

"Only because Grandma Lavish always talked about it," I said. Mostly, I remembered Bible stories like the one about the Ten Commandments. And that story about Adam and Eve. And David. I remember him killing that big giant, Goliath.

"Well, neither had I till she told me. It's the one where Jesus talks about a man who owns a lot of property and has a bunch of money. He's the master. And he goes on a really long trip. Before he leaves for the trip, he calls together his three main servants and gives them each some money. A lot of money. They were called talents. Talents were money then. Instead of dollars, they called them talents. And a talent was big money. One talent was worth something like fifteen years of pay for a mill worker. So that would be about five hundred thousand dollars—a half million bucks—today.

"Well, this master had lots of money. So he gave five talents to one servant. That's two and a half million dollars. Wow, right? To the second servant he gave two talents, a million dollars. And to the third servant, one talent, a half million. Jesus said that he gave them the money based on their ability.

"Then the master left and went on his trip.

"Two of the servants took the big money and used it and made a bunch more money. I don't know what they did, but they doubled their money. Maybe they invested or started businesses or something. But they made more money. The third servant, though, did not. He was scared he was going to lose the money and not have anything when the master came back. So he buried his half million dollars in the ground and hid it so it would be safe.

"Anyway, after a long time, the master came back. And the servants showed up to tell him what they had done. When the first two servants told him that they had doubled the investment money, the master smiled and said, 'Well done, good and faithful servants!' He was one very happy master.

"But when the third servant said he had buried the money because he was scared, the master got angry. That servant had done nothing, and it made the master as mad as a boiled owl. He had given him the money for a purpose. And the servant had done nothing with it. So the master threw the servant out. Forever."

Grandpa stopped again. He leaned over and spit out his wad of tobacco, the whole chunk, into the can. He did this the same way every time. He would spit out the chunk, get some water and rinse his mouth, rub his finger around his gums and teeth, and then spit out the water too. Then, he opened the pack and pulled out some more tobacco strings.

I loved that smell. The taste made me throw up. But the smell of that sweet brown tobacco made my nose smile every time. I guess it just reminded me of Grandpa.

When his mouth was full again, he got back to the story.

"Your Grandma Lavish shared that parable with me, and she said, 'Tommy, do you get it?' And I just shook my head.

"I'm an engineer, Christopher. I like numbers and figures and fixing stuff. I had been sweeping floors all day in a hot cotton mill. I really didn't care much about her story from Jesus. But I loved her. And she loved to pray and read the Bible. So I listened.

"Grandma Lavish kept going. 'I can't believe you don't get it, Tommy. It's so simple. Everything you have God gives to you. And when you make money, it's because God gave you the ability to do something. You're smart at math, and you'll make money with that once you finish at Tech. You work hard. But God gave you the smarts in the first place, Tommy. Your gifts belong to Him. He invested them in you while you're here. And He wants you to produce a return on what He has given you. When you make money with your abilities, it's His. And you'll answer to Him for how you use it, just like the servants did. It all belongs to God. Get it?'

"I nodded and said, 'I suppose so, Lavish. Is this everything you did today while that old lady slept? Didn't you clean her kitchen or bake some cookies, or something?'

"But Grandma Lavish shot back at me, 'I mostly thought today, Tommy. Thought about how God has given you and me the ability to make money and to help people. We can love people by using our money to help them. You and I have a lot of gifts, Tommy. You're smart, and I've always been able to work hard and make money. Do you remember when I sold pieces of gum at school? I paid a penny for each piece and sold it for two pennies. Doubled my money just like those servants in the parable.

"'And when Mom and Dad gave me that corner in the garden, I grew tomatoes and strawberries. They let me keep what I grew in my corner, and I sold that stuff in town at my little table. Do you remember that? I made a lot of money for a kid.

"'While I was reading this parable today, and listening to God, He just made it obvious to me. He already made it clear He wants me to love people as much as I can. And one of the ways I can do that is by using the money I make with the abilities He has given me. Just like the servants in the parable. He loves me and gives me gifts, and I can love people by giving the results of those gifts to them. That means I'm using His investment in me in the right way.

"'If I earn as much as I can, I will be able to help lots of people. Instead of making money for me or for you, I can help kids go to school who wouldn't be able to afford it. I can help families have homes who aren't able to have one on their own. I can help our church because the priest and so many people touch lives that I could never do on my own.

"'It makes sense, Tommy. So I decided I'm gonna love all I can by earning all the money I can and using it to help other people and God's Church.'"

When Grandpa finished that sentence, he took a deep breath. I knew something was coming, but I wasn't sure what. He had a funny look on his face. I didn't say anything. I just waited.

Grandpa looked at me and continued, "Christopher, that woman was a lot of work. She was always about three steps out ahead of me. Felt like I was always running to catch up with her next thought. But I knew I loved her. In fact, I knew God wanted me to marry her and raise kids with her. So I figured out right quick and right there that she was gonna get notions that might not make much sense to me at first, but we were in this together and we would make it work somehow.

"I mean, really. Think about it. This idea was beyond silly. Here I was, a student in college. I had zero money, Christopher. Zero. I was sweeping floors in the summer to help pay for crackers and cheese to eat up in Atlanta at Georgia Tech when I went back to school. I was concerned about getting my education and paying my bills. But your grandmother was already thinking about loving God and loving people. She was light years ahead of me. And I loved her for that. Didn't always make sense to me, but I loved her for that.

"We made a good pair. I fixed things and worked hard. She saw things and pointed the way. We just fit together like a key and a lock.

"So when she said we would earn all we could so we could love God and love people, I just nodded my head and agreed. No use arguing about it. Either we would get married and start working and make money, and she would be right; or I would not be able to graduate, struggle to find a job and be broke, and she would be wrong. But there was no use arguing about it.

"We decided together to earn all we could. But Grandma Lavish just was not going to stop there."

When Grandpa said that, some of my memories made more sense to me now. I always knew Grandma Lavish's favorite parable of Jesus was the parable of the talents. She liked to tell me that the story was really about money. "'Talents' was an old word for money, Christopher." Grandma Lavish said all the money she ever had really belonged to God, and that He expected her to use it wisely. So she worked hard to earn as much money as she could to use that money to love people. *Earn all you can.*

Now I knew where the *E* on the bracelet came from, but Grandpa still didn't give me back my bracelet. Football practice would be starting soon. That meant I wouldn't have much time to sit and listen anymore. If I was gonna find out everything about Grandma Lavish and the bracelet, I needed Grandpa to talk now.

8: THE MITE

Grandpa was missing Grandma Lavish and so was I. My insides hurt from missing her so much. But listening to him talk about her made me feel good, and talking about her made him feel good. It made me feel better, kind of like she was still around in a way. So I started trying to stop in at least once a day just to be with him and listen.

Sometimes, we would sit and watch baseball or talk about my Little League play-offs. I played shortstop, and that made him proud. Especially when I made the all-star team and got to ride on the bus to play in Tampa. Other times, he would sit in that chair and just motion at me to sit on the floor. I knew what that meant. He was in the mood to talk, which meant I quickly got in the mood to listen.

I loved hearing about how he and Grandma Lavish had met, and everything that happened after they got married. But I think her death was doing something way down deep inside him. He seemed different now, without her. I loved to hear the stories, but Grandpa really wanted to focus on Grandma Lavish and that bracelet. And that's what I wanted to hear, so I was glad that's what he wanted to talk about. Plus I just wanted to be near him.

It turned out that they got married once Grandpa finished college at Georgia Tech. I already told you that in the beginning. It took a while before they could have kids, but the first of those was my dad. That's how I got here, you know?

They moved to Orlando after they got married. That's where Grandpa got his first job—working in a mill, but this time as one of the engineers who made sure all the machines worked just right. He ordered new machines, and he fixed the old ones. He watched as people used the equipment to be sure that everything worked like it was supposed to.

Grandpa liked his work in Orlando. But Grandma Lavish was lonely. She didn't like being so far away from Lake Bobola. This was her first time living away from all her people. She struggled to make new friends. Until they found St. Joseph's.

Grandma Lavish needed a prayer chapel in her new town of Orlando. She already had one back home in Lake Bobola, but Orlando was new turf for her and she needed to pray. She didn't mind praying at home, but she wanted a special place where she could sit alone and really concentrate on praying. A place to focus. Stare at Jesus and the crucifix, read her Bible, and listen to God—all that stuff that was so important to her. That's where St. Joseph's came in.

Grandpa and Grandma Lavish lived near one church. I think it was called Immaculate Heart of Mary, and it was in a new building. Grandpa liked to joke that everything in Orlando was new. Disney World didn't even exist yet, but folks were moving to town as Orlando sprouted new buds like a tomato plant making its way up the trellis in Grandma Lavish's garden. Whenever Grandma Lavish went to pray in that new church, she just got all fidgety. Grandpa said it never felt right. She was used to her old church, St. Catherine's, in Lake Bobola.

Orlando was new; Lake Bobola was old. And St. Catherine's was part of that old stuff that Grandma Lavish found so beautiful.

She worried that she would never find a special prayer place like she had back in Lake Bobola. She mostly prayed in a little corner at home, until she decided to start visiting the different parishes around Orlando to see if any of their chapels "felt right."

Finally, she visited St. Joseph's parish, the first church ever built in Orlando. She said St. Joseph's was simple but lovely. Grandpa described for me the old beautiful church building there. Grandma Lavish just loved it. And it had a little adoration chapel that she could nestle into and make her special prayer place.

A few weeks later, Grandpa and Grandma Lavish began to attend Mass at St. Joseph's. They found their home there. They made friends with other married couples. That gave them a sense of home even though Orlando's definitely not Lake Bobola. Not to mention that they loved Father Paul, the pastor there.

And, Grandpa said, it was Father Paul who added the *G* to Grandma Lavish's LEGS bracelet.

Grandpa hadn't mentioned the bracelet for several days, but when we were talking about Orlando, he gave me the hand motion. I sat down and looked up at him in the chair. He looked even skinnier than usual. And I was hoping he was going to give me back the bracelet that day. But I was too scared to ask him for it.

"Christopher," Grandpa said, "your grandmother loved her prayer and study time at St. Joseph's, but that Father Paul really opened the door for us. I will always remember that one homily.

"We had been living in Orlando about a year or so. Here we are, newlyweds, just getting settled into our life together, and Father Paul laid it on us. I don't think he even knew what was going on, but his words and your grandmother's prayer life came together like two bears hugging each other in the woods.

"I liked my job. Grandma Lavish was starting to feel at home in Orlando, and we were having dreams about what our life together could look like. Kids. A house. All that kind of stuff.

"Then Father Paul told us about the mite. The widow's mite. Ever heard of that one?"

Of course I hadn't. Why did he keep asking me all these Bible questions anyway? I just wanted to hear about Grandma Lavish.

Grandpa didn't even wait for an answer. He just kept talking.

"One day Jesus sat and watched as people walked up to the offering bucket and put money into it right outside the temple. Some rich people went up and placed big money in the bucket. Then a little old lady, kind of like the neighbor lady your grandmother used to sit with, hobbled up to the bucket. She put in one little, teeny-tiny copper coin. They call it a mite. No big deal, really. Might not even be worth a penny today.

"But Jesus told His disciples, 'She put in more than everybody else. The rich people contributed out of their abundance. But the widow gave all she had. Everything she had to live on.'

"Then Father Paul said, 'The size of your giving is not measured by how much you give but by how much is left over after you give. The widow was the most generous giver because she gave everything she had. There was nothing left over. She gave one hundred percent. Imagine that.'

"Well, I looked over at Lavish and I knew what was coming after Mass. I just shook my head. I could see it coming a galaxy away.

"After church, we went to eat lunch at a deli, and she gave me time to get comfortable in my seat with my sandwich. Then she said it. 'Tommy, I hope you heard Father Paul today. He crushed it like a hammer on a nail.'

"I played stupid. Just gave her a look across the table like I had no idea what she was talking about. I didn't even want her to know that I had been paying attention at all.

"Don't get me wrong. I loved her. And I appreciated how she wanted to love all she could. I was good with that. I even was OK with the idea of earning all we could so that we could help other people with the money God blessed us with. It all belongs to God. That made sense to me.

"But when I heard that the widow gave 'all that she had; everything she had to live on,' I just did not want to go there with your Grandma Lavish. Who knew what in the world your grandmother was gonna do with that story?

"Well, it turns out that Grandma Lavish had been reading a magazine the week right before Father Paul told us about the widow's mite. So, there at lunch after Mass, she starts telling me about this woman she read about in that magazine. I loved your grandmother, but I could tell this was going someplace where I was gonna be following her and trying to catch up yet again. I hated that feeling. Made me sick to my stomach just to think about it. I quit eating my lunch right then and just let her talk.

"Anyway, the lady's name was Robbie Russell. She was seventy-seven years old. Every day for thirteen years, Robbie rose at two a.m. to bake her special-recipe cream cheese pound cakes. She baked five or six pound cakes every single day. The ingredients cost her about two dollars per cake. She baked them, then sold them and shipped them to customers all over the country for five dollars per cake. Then she gave every bit of money that she made to the teenager ministry at her church. One hundred percent of the proceeds. All of it. She gave it all.

"In thirteen years, Robbie Russell baked over seven thousand cakes and gave more than twenty thousand dollars to help students experience the love of God in Jesus. She gave all the money away. As your grandmother said, 'Then again, that money really wasn't hers to begin with, was it, Tommy? Remember, it all belongs to God.'

"I hated when she did that. Like I didn't remember the lesson from the parable of the talents. I just nodded my head. And mumbled, 'Uh-huh. The parable of the talents. I remember.'

"Grandma Lavish smiled at me. She knew she had me. I was putty in her hands. Drove me crazy.

"She said, 'Tommy, let's try it.'

"I said, 'Try what? Giving everything we have? Do you plan on actually living in a house or would you like to just pitch a tent somewhere?'

"'No, Tommy. Let's just try giving away ten percent. A lot of folks in the Bible did that. Father Paul suggested that would be a good goal to aim at. He told us to just trust God. Give ten percent away, trust God, and see what happens. Father Paul said if we tried that as a goal, he would guarantee our lives would be full in ways we would never expect. He promised. Let's try it. If we don't make it, we can always set a different goal. But let's at least try.'

"I told her, 'Sweetie, ten percent is a lot of money. Especially when you consider that I am twenty-four years old and we are renting a house with two rooms in it. Just how do you propose that we give ten percent of my salary away?'

"Grandma Lavish did not give up. She got a big tear in her eye. It killed me when she got all weepy on me. That drove me crazy.

"'I told you, Tommy, before you ever asked me to marry you, that we were going to love people all we can. And I told you that you and I are going to earn all we can because God has given us all kinds of ability. We are blessed and we need to be thankful for that. And the only way we are ever going to love all we can with what we earn is if we give all we can. And ten percent is a place to start. Father Paul said so. You were sitting right there. We need to start trying now. It's just too easy to keep putting it off.'

"So I explained to her, 'Now, Lavish, you listen to me. Ten percent is a lot of money. I'm telling you that right now. And in case you haven't noticed, we do not exactly have a lot of money to begin with. You buy the groceries, you pay the bills, and you tell me almost every week, 'Honey, I'm not sure we're gonna make it this week,' in your little high-pitched worried voice. But I tell you what, I will make you a deal. When we get home today, let's get out the check-book and see just how much money we gave away last year. We don't even know. We've never even actually measured it. So let's measure it. We'll add it all up. Because I bet we are way more generous with our money in helping people and the Church than you think we are. In fact, I'll bet you we give away close to ten percent right now. But if somehow we are nowhere near that, you and I will map out a plan to give all we can. We'll set a goal. OK? Deal?'"

That's how it began. Grandpa and Grandma Lavish agreed at lunch after the Mass where Father Paul taught them about the widow who gave all she had that they would give all they could. They even agreed to aim for the ten percent Father Paul had suggested as a goal, since it seemed crazy to try to give everything you had. Nobody could do one hundred percent, but they could at least try to give ten percent.

When they got home, they got out the checkbook and a blank piece of paper. Grandma Lavish read out the amounts of checks that they had given to St. Joseph's parish and to the assistance fund at the Catholic school next door, as well as to Father Rick's orphanage in Haiti, where the little kids needed shoes and Grandma Lavish wanted to help. They also included the check they wrote to buy lunch boxes for the children in the family who lived next door when their father had lost his job for two weeks and had no money to start the school year. Ever since Grandma Lavish had heard about that little boy left all alone in the closet, she wanted to help kids anytime she could.

Grandpa and Grandma Lavish measured their giving to see with their own eyes just how much they actually had given. Grandma Lavish totaled it all up. She and Grandpa had given away $272 that past year. Grandpa made a salary of $16,000 in his new engineering job, so he quickly did the math. They had given away 1.7 percent of their money to love and help people in the past twelve months. He and Lavish were both surprised at how low that percentage was. Especially when they thought about the ten percent that Father Paul had recommended as a goal. Ten percent felt like a long way from 1.7 percent.

"Just trust God," Lavish reminded Grandpa. "That's what Father Paul said. Just. Trust. God."

Grandpa stopped telling me the story. He shook his head. His face got all curled up and twisted. He rubbed his forehead with his hand like a wet rag.

And then he started again. "Christopher, I have to tell you. That was probably the hardest conversation we ever had together. It was a struggle. Worse than the time we couldn't agree on the house we were going to live in. Worse than the time we thought I had a job back in Lake Bobola and then it fell through and your grandmother got so sad that it took me days to convince her that we would eventually make our life together back home one day.

"Nope, this conversation was tough. We both looked at that number and realized that we were not nearly as generous as we thought we were. Worse, we weren't as generous as we wanted to be. I really did want to be generous, Christopher. By then, Grandma Lavish had convinced me that we were doing the right thing. That we really were cooperating with God by trying to love as much as we could and earn as much as we could. But when we actually measured how much we gave, it all became real. And we knew if we didn't set a goal, we'd never change and become generous like we wanted to be.

"It was tough at first, because I was looking at what we didn't have. We were so young, and I was thinking about all the stuff that was going to happen in the years ahead. Kids, house, cars. All that stuff. But I knew deep down that she was right. It all belongs to God. And we needed to give all we could. That was the right thing to do. To love God and to love people. And somehow we needed to write down a plan to at least try to get to the ten percent that Father Paul had recommended as a great goal. We owed it to ourselves, and to God too, I reckon, to at least try. If we didn't make it to ten percent, at least we would know we had really given it a shot.

"Before we made our plan, we talked about Father Cascia again. About his sacrifice to save your grandmother's life. His act reminded us of God. That was the very first time I heard your grandmother say, 'God is the Supreme Giver, and when you give, you become just like Him. Father Cascia gave everything he had, Tommy. He gave 100%. Just like the widow.'

"We both wanted to get there, but I just couldn't see how to do it. So we got out a piece of scrap paper and we sat at the kitchen table. And on the left side of the paper, I wrote down the year. On the right side, I wrote the percentage we would try to give. We decided that if we were at 1.7 percent now, we would just add one percentage point each year until we got to ten."

Grandpa got a piece of paper and made a list. "Here's what it looked like," he said, and he showed me the list.

Year	Percentage
1949	1.7%
1950	2%
1951	3%
1952	4%
1953	5%
1954	6%
1955	7%
1956	8%
1957	9%
1958	10%

"Looking at it that way made it seem like we could do it," he continued. "A little bit at a time. Start with a small step. And then take another small step. Just grow a little bit each year.

"Grandma Lavish and I got excited when we looked at that piece of paper and our plan to be generous. When we wrote it down, we knew we could do it. One little bit of growth at a time.

"I also realized that that was the first time I had ever actually written down goals that had anything to do with God. I had always had plans and goals. In fact, I had plans for everything in my life except God. Everything before that had been all about me: my schooling, my career, my house, my plans. But this was all about God and other people. And I have to tell you, it felt good to focus on God and helping people for a change. Love all you can. Earn all you can. Give all you can.

"It felt so good that we kept talking. We even decided to plan out where we would give the money. Not just how much we were going to give. But to set a goal for the places it would go.

"We wanted our gifts to really love people and help them. And we wanted to please God with the way we were using what He had given us. Just like the servants wanted to please the master in that parable your grandma told me about.

"We did not want our giving to get spread too thin. We decided to try to have a real impact on a few things rather than a very small impact on a lot of things. We focused on

the ministries that meant the most to us. And we asked
God to help us decide.

"We knew that our parish came first. Father Paul and St.
Joseph's had helped us so much that we wanted other people
to be helped in the same way. So we committed that day to
give all our generosity to the parish until we got to the five
percent level, which would occur in our plan by 1950. After
all, St. Joseph's parish was our home. The parish helped lots
of people in need. It provided ministries for children to get
to know Jesus. Plus, it fed us the Eucharist and helped us
know Jesus more deeply ourselves. It just made sense that
our parish came first.

"St. Joseph's meant so much to us, we wanted to express
gratitude to God and His work there."

Grandpa made another list:

1949	1.7% to lots of things
1950	2% to St. Joseph's
1951	3% to St. Joseph's
1952	4% to St. Joseph's
1953	5% to St. Joseph's

Then he continued, "Once we got to that five percent
level, we decided that the next two percent would go to the
orphans in Haiti that Father Rick's ministry helped. They
needed housing, clothing, food, and education. The need
there was so great. And we just knew that God was prod-
ding us to be part of the solution. Helping children in need
always bubbled up to the top of our priorities."

Grandpa added two more things to the list:

1954 : 6% = 5% to St. Joseph's +
 1% to Orphans in Haiti
1955 : 7% = 5% to St. Joseph's +
 2% to Orphans in Haiti

"We believed it was important to invest in our parish because that was our home," he went on. "We believed it was important to give to kids in desperate need, and Father Rick's orphanage served those kids well. Jesus had compassion. And we believed it was important to share our faith with other people, especially children. Making sure that children got inspired by the beauty and genius of the Catholic faith, just like we had been, meant the world to us. That's hope. That was one way we could help make the Church's future even stronger. So we wrote down money for kids to be able to get a Catholic education in Orlando. The next two percent would go to the scholarship fund at the school there. Sharing the faith with others got me excited."

The next thing Grandpa added to his list was:

1956 : 8% = 5% to St. Joseph's
 + 2% to Orphans in Haiti
 + 1% to Scholarship
1957 : 9% = 5% to St. Joseph's
 + 2% to Orphans in Haiti
 + 2% to Scholarship

"Finally," he said, "we decided that the final one percent, the last one that would put us at Father Paul's recommend-

ed goal of ten percent, would be committed year-to-year
based on whatever inspired us or we got excited about.
Sometimes it might be a family in our community who
needed help. Or a mom needing help in the pregnancy re-
source center. Or a missionary who was creating a school
in Senegal. Or the Catholic Refugee Services helping so
many people in Florida then. We would decide how to give
that last one percent each year as needs arose and as we felt
God nudging us. We called this our Nudge Fund because
it would be flexible from year to year. When God nudged,
we'd be ready to give."

And he added the last thing to the list:

> 1958 : 10% = 5% to St. Joseph's
> + 2% to Orphans in Haiti
> + 2% to Scholarship
> + 1% to Nudge Fund

"All of a sudden, when we wrote down our giving plan,
Christopher, it became real and it became fun. I loved it. I
could see on paper where the money was going, and I could
envision in my mind the lives who would be better because
of it. Thinking about how we could use our money in the
highest and best ways to love God and to love people. Help.
Compassion. Hope. It didn't feel like a struggle anymore. It
felt great.

"Writing it down on paper was the best thing we ever did.
It made it real. I could see the goals. Best of all, I could see
the lives that would be touched by our gifts.

"That was what surprised me most. Once Grandma Lavish got me going, I actually looked forward to talking about giving all we could. I even loved to write those checks. I saw the ways that people would be helped and loved. And I knew that your grandmother was on to something big. And something special. *Give all you can.*

"But I never envisioned where the road to giving would take us. I wasn't used to giving, but I grew into it faster than I ever thought. But the best was yet to come."

I wasn't sure what Grandpa meant by that, but I was thinking he had to be referring to what happened that time when Benson Norris went crazy in downtown Lake Bobola.

The Tom & Lavish Grace
Family Giving Plan

1949:   1.7% to lots of things
1950:   2% to St. Joseph's
1951:   3% to St. Joseph's
1952:   4% to St. Joseph's
1953:   5% to St. Joseph's
1954:   6% = 5% to St. Joseph's
              + 1% to Orphan's in Haiti
1955%   7% = 5% to St. Joseph's
              + 2% to Orphans in Haiti
1956:   8% = 5% to St. Joseph's
              + 2% to Orphans in Haiti
              + 1% to Scholarship
1957%   9% = 5% to St. Joseph's
              + 2% to Orphans in Haiti
              + 2% to Scholarship
1958%   10% = 5% to St. Joseph's
              + 2% to Orphans in Haiti
              + 1% to Scholarship
              + 1% Nudge Fund

9: THE BLESSING

Lake Bobola is small, but it's not that small. I mean, we're bigger than Frostproof. Just about every place is bigger than Frostproof. But we're smaller than Tampa and Orlando, and all those other big places in Florida everybody has heard of.

We have a really nice downtown, where I ride my bike. We've got a movie theater and some stores. And a couple of banks. We're the main town in this part of Florida, so we have the big courthouse too. There's always a bunch of people around that.

We may be small, but when Lake Bobola makes the news, we do it big. And a few years ago, every TV station in the country was here to follow the big shootout at our courthouse. You probably remember it. It was the one where Benson Norris escaped out of handcuffs, stole a guard's gun, and started shooting anybody and everybody who got in his way.

I didn't know Benson Norris, but I saw him on TV. He was big. Like NFL big. And mean, like scary movie mean. He had been in jail a couple of times for all kinds of bad stuff. He had robbed some people, hit a guy in the head with his gun, stolen some cars. Lots of things. My dad said he didn't understand it because Benson Norris was a smart man who had gone to college and had gotten some good jobs. I just said he was mean, and some people are like that. Scared me just to look at him on the TV.

Well, Benson Norris was at the courthouse, and they had him all locked up in shackles and everything. Guards were protecting him and waiting for his turn to go into the courtroom. I never did hear if he was on trial or going in there for something else. Either way, he never made it.

Somehow, Benson got alone with one guard, a woman. And he was able to get her gun and the key to his shackles. And before you knew it, Benson Norris had shot that guard, and then he ran into the courtroom and shot the judge and another lady right in the head. She was just sitting there typing stuff, and he shot her right in the head. Why would anybody be that mean?

He killed them all, but he was just getting started. Benson was determined to get away, so he started running. He knew his way around the courthouse pretty good. He'd been there a lot. So he ran down the back stairs, and got out into the street. I mean, there's this crazy escaped guy with a gun, wearing that bright orange prison suit, standing right in the downtown square of Lake Bobola. I'm glad I wasn't in town that day to buy baseball cards or something. Can you imagine how scared everybody was?

So Benson Norris started looking for a getaway car. He pulled a lady out of her car and threw her into the street. He jumped in and started to speed off when Officer Harry Beasley ran out of the courthouse and into the street to try to stop him. My friends told me that Officer Beasley pulled out his gun and aimed it at that car with Benson Norris in it, but before he could pull the trigger, Benson fired and hit Officer Beasley right in the chest.

People were running everywhere, trying to get away from all that mess. I mean, it was crazy. Benson Norris drove away and left big old skid marks in the street. And Officer Beasley died right there in the middle of the street in front of the courthouse in downtown Lake Bobola. Right in the middle of where Orange Street runs into Broad. I've been by there a million times before and since. You can still see a little spot of blood on the pavement if you look close enough.

So that's four people dead in Lake Bobola, including a judge and two officers. All by one crazy guy. I told you he was mean. And ugly too.

That's why all the TV newspeople showed up. Benson Norris got away and he was on the run for three whole days. Nobody knew where he was. They looked everywhere. Meanwhile, all the TV people were downtown with their big vans and satellite dishes, and most of them kept looking around every time they made an announcement because they were all scared he'd come right back to the courthouse and do some more shooting just to make his point. This guy was crazy. Really. My dad made me stay home the whole time.

Anyway, Benson Norris turned himself in after those three days. He had gone to a woman's apartment and was hiding at her place. She said he just showed up in the parking lot, and asked for a place to stay. She said she knew who he was. She recognized him from TV. She was scared to death. I would've been too. He stayed at her house for two whole days. He knew the roads were blocked, and there was no way he was gonna be able to get out of Beverley County.

The lady he stayed with said he was real nice the whole time he was there. Just asked her to fix him some scrambled eggs and some grits and stuff. And then he called the police, walked out into the parking lot of the apartments, and turned himself in. He's in jail now. That's where he belongs. For the rest of his life. He was crazy mean.

Well, our priest, Father Fisher, watched all this on the news too. He was one of the chaplains at the jail and the courthouse, so he knew all the people who got shot. The judge and the lady in the courtroom. The woman guard. And Officer Harry Beasley. The shooting happened on Tuesday, and Benson Norris didn't turn himself in until Friday. But when he saw what had happened, Father Fisher knew what he needed to do at the Masses on Saturday and Sunday at St. Catherine's parish.

On Sunday, Father Fisher shared with all of us what had happened. (Like anybody in Lake Bobola would not have heard about it or something!) He said he had been praying about how our church should help. He said we are a people of hope, and he believed God had made it clear to him. He invited us to make a gift, to honor the four dead people and to help the family of Officer Harry Beasley.

Our priest knew Officer Beasley. He also knew a sheriff's deputy didn't make much money. Dad said the judge and the lady who worked in the courtroom both had good insurance policies and their kids were grown. The lady officer was single and had no kids. But Officer Beasley was married and had two daughters. One, Deandra, was eight. The other, Deidre, was five. And somehow the family had to figure out how to pay for their house, and to raise those girls, and to help them go to college, and lots of stuff. So Father Fisher asked us to make a special gift for Mrs. Beasley that day. He passed the offering baskets around right toward the end of Mass. He said that every penny given would help the Beasley family raise those girls and pay for their house since their daddy had died trying to do what was right. Officer Beasley was brave and he was a hero.

I was little. I think I was five then, but I still remember that offering. Father Fisher was crying. It was like his heart was breaking just thinking about all those dead people and that one crazy mean man, Benson Norris. Father Fisher wanted us to help, and he told us that we would become better people by giving. That we would be heroes too. "People of hope," he kept saying over and over.

Then Father Fisher told us about a man in the parish named Aldred. Actually, his whole name was Aldred Pruden Jenkins. That's a weird name for a man. Aldred lived his last eighteen months in a nursing home. Father Fisher said Aldred only had a little money that he got in a pension check every month. "He had no possessions but he possessed a wonderful, warm, and generous spirit," he said. I liked how he said that.

The staff at the nursing home loved Aldred and would do anything for him. In his last few months, he became really confused and wasn't able to think clearly. The staff said Aldred created different pretend situations in his mind. One day he even said that the President of the United States had consulted him for advice on Saudi Arabia. But most of the pretend situations revolved around money. Like, old man Aldred thought he had two hundred million dollars left over from World War II. He said he really wanted to do nice things for his friends and the people who took care of him at the nursing home.

So several times a day, Aldred would walk up to a nurse or the lady who served him his food. He'd pull them aside and whisper in their ear, "I want to give you a million dollars because you've been so kind, so good to me." The nursing home staff would chuckle every time Aldred's son came to visit. They would smile and say, "Your dad has been so generous with his money!"

Then Father Fisher said that one day they found Aldred very quiet and sitting off all by himself. He never did that. And he was like that for several days in a row. Then he died. It turned out he'd had a stroke, and no one really knew it. The stroke changed him. His smiling face turned into a big frown. And he did not want to be around people anymore.

The nurse said, "We knew something was wrong. When he quit giving, we knew something was clearly wrong."

Right then, Father Fisher shouted to us, "I hope that you and I become so generous in this life that when we stop giving, someone will notice and say, 'Surely something must be wrong!'"

When he said that, Grandma Lavish got out her checkbook. She just nodded her head; didn't say a word. I was sitting right next to her. Me, Mom, Dad, and Grandpa. We were all there. Little Michael was in the nursery, I think. He cried a lot, so he stayed in the nursery when we went to Mass.

Everybody in the whole church stood up when Father Fisher passed the baskets that second time. They clapped and cheered. Really, we all did! We all wanted to help. Who wouldn't want to help a hero's family? And who wouldn't want to be a hero too? Anyway, a couple of days later, Grandma Lavish told me how much all the people gave that day. I don't remember numbers that big. It was bigger than any number I had ever heard of, but I believed her.

I've been to Mass a lot of times, and I've never seen people stand up and clap during the offering. That just never happens. It was like being at the Florida Gators football games. My dad likes to take me to those sometimes. And that's what this felt like. People were excited to give. It was different than church usually felt.

Two weeks later, Father Fisher invited Mrs. Beasley and her two girls to come to Mass. They weren't Catholic, so they got a little confused at some of the kneeling and stuff, but they sat up front. Right there on the first pew. Nobody ever sits there, but Mrs. Beasley and Deandra and Deidre did. I guess they didn't know nobody does that.

And at the end of Mass, after the Eucharist, Father Fisher asked everybody to sit down. He told Mrs. Beasley to come up front and stand by him. Father Fisher told her and everybody there what we had done. He said, "The people of St. Catherine's loved your husband very much. And we were very proud of him for being a hero. And we love you too. And we want to help you. So we would like to give you this check. I am proud to tell St. Catherine's that this check is big enough to pay for the Beasleys' whole house once and for all. No more house payments for the Beasley family. Never again. And there is enough left over to put ten thousand dollars in two accounts. One for Deandra's college fund, and one for Deidre's. God bless you and your husband's memory."

I remember those words. And I also remember that Grandma Lavish had big tears rolling down her cheeks. Everybody did. Everybody had given. It was like we were one big giant family all doing the same thing at the same time. It was crazy. Not Benson Norris mean crazy but a good crazy. "People of hope" crazy, I guess you could call it.

Mrs. Beasley couldn't even speak. She just stood there and nodded her head. Her lips tried to say "Thank you," but nothing came out. They just trembled. Then everybody stood up and clapped for her and her girls. Even Grandpa cried.

Clapping and cheering two times in Mass. And I was there for both of them. It's never happened again. Probably won't either. But Grandma Lavish told me when we got home from Mass, "Christopher, today was the proudest I have ever been to be a Christian. I'm glad you were with me to see it. That was our church at her best. Remember that."

And then she gave me a big hug. It was a good day.

Give all you can. Grandma Lavish liked to say, "Use money and love people. Don't ever get that backwards, Christopher." I think seeing the Beasley family that day in church was the first time I ever understood what Grandma Lavish meant by that. Because that day the church was full of nothing but love. And hope.

10: THE CAKES

Grandma Lavish liked to do what she did best: She baked cakes. Strawberry cakes just like her own grandmother had taught her using that secret recipe.

I knew that part of the story. We had talked about it ever since I was born. I even went down to her bakery at least once a week. But you don't know about that part yet.

When they got married, Grandpa worked. I told you that. And while he was at work, Grandma Lavish wanted something to do. She wasn't sure she liked living in Orlando, so she figured it would be best if she kept herself busy. So she did what she did best. She baked.

That's how it got started—a summer project, before they had kids. And Grandma Lavish figured she'd do it while they were in Orlando, until they moved back to Lake Bobola.

Now, I don't have to tell you that Grandma Lavish did not need to try very hard to sell her cakes. Everybody wanted them. People just came to her. Her cakes were really that good. I wish you could've tasted them for yourself. You'd love them.

People wanted her cakes for birthday parties, stuff at work . . . Grandma Lavish said men even stopped by to get cakes because they wanted a treat for their wives. You get the picture. Once everybody knew Grandma Lavish was making her cakes every day, they showed up and wanted to buy them. It wasn't long before her strawberry cakes became famous. I bet everybody in Orlando knew about them.

Grandma Lavish told me all about it one day while we were sitting in the kitchen. We were waiting for Grandpa to get home from the hardware store so we could eat lunch. He was taking longer than usual that Saturday, so Grandma Lavish just started talking about her baking. I'm not sure why. I guess she just wanted me to know how it all got started.

In the beginning, she could buy all the stuff for her famous strawberry cake for two dollars. And while Grandpa worked at the mill during the day, she could bake five cakes, every day.

She sold her cakes for five dollars easy. That meant she made a profit of three whole dollars for every cake that she baked. She liked to think of herself as being just like Robbie Russell, that old lady she had read about in the magazine article, the one who baked cream cheese pound cakes.

Well, that was a lot of money. I could buy a bunch of baseball cards with that. Three dollars profit for five cakes every day. That's, like, fifteen dollars. But Grandma Lavish didn't buy baseball cards. She put that money in the bank. She started a brand-new, special bank account. She called it the Cascia account. That was named after Father Frank Cascia, who I told you about. The priest who saved her from drowning when she was a little girl. Remember?

Anyway, Grandma Lavish was really proud of that bank account. The more she thought about Robbie Russell, the more she wanted to be like her. She thought about that little boy over in Tampa who had nobody and had nothing to eat except peanut butter on his bare hands. She thought about how she could give a little help and some hope to kids like that. So Grandma Lavish saved all that money from baking strawberry cakes so she could use it to love people. She didn't spend any of it on herself at all. I probably would have. I'd have bought a new bike, and probably a baseball glove too.

Don't get me wrong. I would've given some, but she wanted to give it all. She and Grandpa knew they could live on the money Grandpa made at the mill. And they were already trying to make their goal of giving away ten percent of his salary just like they had talked about. But Grandma Lavish wanted to do even more. If you knew her, you'd understand better. She was just like that. She said baking allowed her to do just what God wanted her to do: earn more, give more, and love more. She smiled when she told me that.

Grandma Lavish knew she could bake; heck, everybody knew she could bake. So she just started doing it. And pretty soon, she was a big deal.

She called her strawberry cakes Cascia Cakes, to remember Father Cascia. She loved to call her money "Cascia Cash." She grinned every time she said it. And every time she put money in that account, she said her heart felt bigger.

She wanted to honor Father Cascia and the way he had shown her how real love sacrifices.

One time, when I asked Grandpa about the Cascia Cakes, he chuckled and said, "Every time she sold one, your Grandma Lavish would wink at me and say, 'Tommy, you and I are earning and loving all we can.'" Everybody knew her grin turned on a room like a light switch.

Well, it wasn't long before those Cascia Cakes made her bank account all full and everything. I mean, think about it. Fifteen dollars a day. Times five days a week. That's seventy-five dollars every week in money that Grandma Lavish could begin giving away. And that was just at the start. I haven't even told you the best part yet.

Grandpa told me that seventy-five dollars a week was a huge amount of money back then. And he reminded me that before they made their giving plan, he and Grandma Lavish gave away $272 in one year. Now she could give that much money away every month just by baking! Grandma Lavish was amazing, wasn't she?

Well, sometime in there, she decided to make a little rubber bracelet. Grandpa said she wanted one kind of like the one Father Cascia had been wearing when he rescued her. The one he was wearing on the boat and the one he got buried in. I guess she wanted to wear a little reminder. Only thing was, she didn't put "LOVE" on it like Father Cascia had. Instead, Grandma Lavish put her own special letters: "LEGS."

Love.

Earn.

Give.

Save.

Grandpa said Grandma Lavish started her day the same way every time back then. She would get up at seven o'clock, eat a ham biscuit or some eggs, turn on her music in the kitchen, put on her LEGS bracelet, and set up for her day of baking five strawberry cakes.

Remember how I told you that Grandpa and Grandma Lavish eventually moved back to Lake Bobola and started their family? Well, when they finally were able to have children, she kept right on baking just the same. Then they had my dad. Then three more children. And Grandma Lavish just baked right around them. Some days lots of cakes; some days, not so many. But she was always baking. Her baking was just part of the family. And so was her giving.

Grandpa always wrote a check to St. Catherine's at the start of each month for the five percent of his paycheck, just like they had promised. They had done that when they were at St. Joseph's, and now that they were back home in Lake Bobola, they kept up the same habit by giving to St. Catherine's. That was the first part of their giving plan. And they stuck to it. After they got to five percent, then they started giving money to Father Rick's orphanage in Haiti. Then they started to give the scholarship money to the little Catholic school here in Lake Bobola, where I go. Grandpa was real proud of that. He likes plans and goals. He makes one for their garden every year. I've seen it. So, when they had their plan for giving, he was not gonna stop until they reached their ten percent goal. And they did it.

Because Grandma Lavish sold so many cakes, she and Grandpa got all kinds of money to help people with. Grandpa said it was so much fun because her Cascia money helped them give over and above their giving plan. When a single mom got the news that she had breast cancer, Grandpa and Grandma Lavish used their Cascia Cash to pay her doctor bills. When a young man in town who didn't know his daddy wanted to go to college, my grandparents wrote the checks. Grandpa even told me how one day in the grocery store, Grandma Lavish watched a mother going all crazy with her three children and a grocery cart filled with fruit, vegetables, and cereal. When the cashier rang up that lady's total, she told her oldest boy to take some of the groceries back because they did not have enough money to buy everything they had in the cart. But Grandma Lavish stepped in and told the cashier, "I'll pay the whole bill. Please bag this woman's food, and we'll help her get to the car." I wish I could've seen that mother's face. Grandpa said it swelled with tears.

Grandpa said it changed everything when he and Grandma Lavish saw that everything belongs to God. They quit worrying so much. They said thank you more. Giving became fun. Grandpa said it made him feel like he was doing some good in the world.

Then came the Beverley County fair of 1986. Just a couple of years before I was born. I love the fair. I'm not sure which part I enjoy most. It's probably the spinning Ferris wheel that turns you upside down and all around as it goes in that big circle. I threw up in that one time. Mom got mad at me, but I couldn't help it. What I really like is the shooting booth where you win prizes by hitting the little metal ducks as they move in front of you. I'm a good shooter. I even won a big stuffed Pink Panther.

Grandma Lavish decided it would be fun to spend a whole week in October selling her cakes at the fair. I'm not sure why she thought about that. But she did. She not only decided to sell her famous strawberry Cascia Cakes. But for the first time, she made strawberry cupcakes. Now, that is a perfect snack at the fair. I love cupcakes.

Sales at the fair went great. Grandma Lavish set up her own stand right between the Kiwanis Club's hot dog and hamburger grill and the guy with the cotton candy machine. She got ready ahead of time. She baked extra cakes and froze them weeks before the fair.

Grandpa said that on Monday and Tuesday Grandma Lavish sold ten cakes each day. But the unbelievable part was that she sold two hundred cupcakes to all the hungry kids and their parents. I wish I could've been there. Two hundred! Her cupcakes became the hit of the whole fair.

Strawberry cupcake sales exploded because the first people who saw them told everybody that now you could buy Grandma Lavish's famous Cascia Cakes as little cupcakes. On Wednesday and Thursday, sales doubled to four hundred cupcakes per day. Grandpa said it was out of control. There were lines at her table; she was running out of cakes. Can you believe it? Grandma Lavish had had no idea that the fair was gonna be like a rocket launching pad for her Cascia Cakes. But, like Grandpa said, the rocket was just getting off the ground.

Sales were totally crazy on Saturday and Sunday, when crowds were the biggest. I always spend the whole day Saturday at the fair. All the kids do. They did the same thing even back then. Grandma Lavish had to get somebody to help her keep up with all the customers.

By the end of the fair, Grandma Lavish had sold more than two hundred of her regular strawberry cakes, and who knows how many millions and millions of cupcakes. Grandpa said they had actually lost count. But Grandma Lavish did know this: She now had more than four thousand dollars to put in her Cascia account. That was her biggest deposit ever! It was more than she could make in a whole year with her regular baking. And she did it in just one week.

That's when Sam Winston did something really crazy. Word of Grandma Lavish's delicious Cascia Cakes spread all over the place after the fair. People came to the Beverley County fair from as far away as Texas and Kansas. And they told everybody what had happened in Lake Bobola. About how they had tasted these incredible strawberry delights. When they went home, they wanted to buy more cakes to be shipped to them. Grandma Lavish went crazy and didn't know what to do. She couldn't keep up with all these folks who wanted her cakes. As Grandpa said, she was just one lady in her own little kitchen, with a family to care for; it was amazing.

Well, anyway, Sam Winston owned lots and lots of land around Lake Bobola. He still does. He even ran a bunch of trucks that drove stuff all across the country. He's really rich. Grandpa said Sam Winston liked to do things big. He saw all the success at the fair and offered to help Grandma Lavish. He knew she had said that she wanted to earn all she could so she could love and give all she could.

So Sam went up to Grandma Lavish and asked her, "How many cakes would you really like to make each week?"

Grandma Lavish looked a little surprised. "What are you talking about, Sam?"

"Well, I know that you could sell as many cakes and cupcakes as you can make. The real question is how much do you want to work at this? You've got four kids now and grandchildren will be showing up before you know it. That's your first priority. And Tom makes a good salary. So you are not pressed for money. Let's figure out what you really want to do. You've inspired me. You've got passion and fire. Your giving helps a lot of people. I want to help you.

"I'll let you set up in one of my warehouses for free. If you'd like, I'll help you hire a few people and put in some large ovens to make it happen, if you want this thing to get a little bigger than just you in your kitchen between ball games and homework with your kids. But you have to decide, Lavish, how big you are willing to let this thing get. It's your life."

So Grandpa and Grandma Lavish decided to sit down with Sam Winston and make a new plan. They told him how their plan was not really about Cascia Cakes but about LEGS. She told Sam how she wanted to love all she could, earn all she could, give all she could, and save all she could.

Generosity was her goal. She didn't want to have a huge business or become famous. And she didn't want a bunch of headaches that came with all that stuff. No, Grandma Lavish wanted to care for her family and also use her gifts to love people completely. That had always been her plan. Grandpa made enough to support the family and give ten percent. That meant Grandma Lavish could love, earn, and give as much as she wanted.

Grandpa said they all decided that a good size would be a bakery that would allow her to make five hundred dollars per week in Cascia cash to give away. She liked that idea. With some people to help her run it, she could stop in and be sure things were done the way she wanted. But she could also focus first on her family. Grandpa said it was the best of both worlds. Grandma Lavish could love her family and still give people the joy of a tasty strawberry cake. Best of all, she could give people love by sharing the money she made in the ways that God nudged her. She loved that word, **nudge.** She always waited for God's nudge when she was praying or being asked to give to something.

So that's the story of how, after years of getting up every day and baking five cakes per day, my grandmother, Mrs. Lavish Grace, moved all her baking out of her kitchen and into a building owned by Mr. Sam Winston. And he did just what he had promised. He helped her buy new machines, kind of like the ones Grandpa took care of at the mill. Only these machines baked cakes instead of making towels.

Grandma Lavish named her little business LEGS Baking. She even made LEGS bracelets for everybody who worked there. She wanted everybody to remember Father Cascia and why they were baking cakes: to love.

Pretty soon, people just started showing up to help. Most of them didn't even want to get paid. Grandpa said people just want to be around a lady who is so generous and so loving. They popped up nearly every day to pack boxes or run cakes around town just to help.

It was like my grandmother became a love magnet. We studied magnets in science last year. You set a magnet on your desk, and all the little pieces of metal fly to it and stick. Grandma Lavish was like that. Only it was people who flew to her. I wanted to be near her too.

But I never knew her magnetic power stretched all the way to a trash dump.

11: THE CROWD

Summer was coming to a close. And that meant I had to go back to school. But before I did, I wanted to spend as much time with Grandpa as I could. Kind of like when I sit on the beach on our last night of vacation each year. I like to stay out there until every last bit of the sunset is gone from the sky. That way I know vacation is really completely over for another year.

With only a little time left before school was back in session, I started to pop by Grandpa's house most every day. I wanted to enjoy each moment of my time with him. Plus, he still had my bracelet. I really wanted to be able to wear it when school started.

On Monday of that last week, I rode up on my bike in the middle of the morning, probably about ten o'clock. I walked up the steps and found him on the front porch this time. Usually he liked to be inside by now so he would not be sitting out in the sun as the day started getting hot. But there he was, gently swaying in the front porch swing.

Grandpa loved that swing. Most evenings, he would sit in it for at least a few minutes, no matter what time of year it was. Sometimes he sat there for the whole evening. It usually depended on baseball. If a game was on TV, he'd be inside watching it from his big brown recliner. If there was no game on, he'd be outside enjoying that swing. I liked to climb up in it, even when I was just three or four, and sit next to him for what seemed like the whole day. I loved that spot—sitting next to Grandpa as we moved back and forth.

Seeing him on the porch at ten o'clock in the morning surprised me a little bit. He was doing his normal thing. Sitting in the swing, spitting tobacco juice over his shoulder each time he swung back. Grandma Lavish hated that. She would yell at him from inside the house, "Tommy, you'd better not be spitting your nasty old tobacco juice in the middle of my yard." It really made her mad that their front yard had a big dead spot in it, right where the tobacco spit landed each time Grandpa shot it out of his mouth from that swing up on the porch.

I sat in the swing next to him; my familiar spot. And I asked him, "Grandpa, can we talk about the funeral some more? And can I please have the bracelet back?"

"Uh-huh. What's on your mind, Christopher?" He reached into his pocket and pulled out the LEGS bracelet. He handed it to me. I kind of expected him to say something about it, but he didn't. I wondered if he had been keeping that bracelet in his pocket ever since he had asked me for it.

I put the bracelet back on my wrist, and told him about the man I wanted to hear more about. "Well, I've been thinking about the stories you've been telling me. About your life with Grandma Lavish. About the bracelet. About the people y'all helped. About your giving. And I was wondering about a man I met at the funeral. His name was Gilbert. Do you know him?"

"Of course I know Gilbert, Christopher. He wrote your grandmother notes nearly every week. Why? What did he say to you?"

"Well, he said he wanted to come just to say thanks. That he loved Grandma Lavish. And he said I had some big shoes to fill when I grow up. How do y'all know him?" Grandpa spit out some tobacco juice as the swing hit its highest point. Then he started talking again.

"I only met Gilbert in person a couple of times. He's from Haiti. But I read his letters. At first, they were written in French or Creole or something, so I had to get some help from a teacher at the high school to be able to read them. But later, he learned English, and that made it easier for me to understand his notes.

"Gilbert was two years old when his mother got sick, real sick. He never knew his father. I'm not sure what the deal was on that. But his mother got sick, and she knew she had to find a place for Gilbert to live in case she died. That happens a lot in Haiti. And it happened to Gilbert.

"She was not a rich woman. In fact, she lived by the garbage dump. That way, she could pick through other people's trash in hopes of finding enough food to feed herself and her little son, Gilbert. The sad thing is, Christopher, she was not alone. There was a whole village of people living under pieces of fabric and surviving on the scraps of food they found as they dug through the dump. They lived right beside a huge heap of trash. Amazing.

"Gilbert's mom visited Father Rick and his orphanage several times. She asked questions about the home and what the kids did there and whether they got to go to school. She even said that she hoped Gilbert could live there after she died. She really wanted to live. I'm not sure she ever believed the doctors who told her how sick she was.

"Anyway, Father Rick said he knew one of the men who worked the night patrol out by the dump. His name was Jacques.

One night, Jacques was training a new partner on the evening patrol when the rookie said, 'Did you hear that, Jacques? You better come take a look.' The rookie pointed toward the edge of the dump. The nasty stench of that garbage filled the air and Jacques's nose, even though he was used to it; he'd been patrolling this area for years.

"Jacques stepped through piles of rotten fruit and vegetables, over a broken wooden school chair, and into a disgusting pile of trash that was so far gone, he couldn't even identify most of it. There were decaying pieces of corn and beans and some balls of rotting cabbage. In the middle of that pile, wrapped in a tattered brown towel, was a little boy. And lying next to him was a woman who looked like she had died earlier that day. The little boy was breathing very heavy, and Jacques was not sure how much longer he had to live.

"That's when Jacques called Father Rick. And that's how Gilbert came into our lives. Being found by the dump by the night patrol had saved his life. He arrived at the orphanage at the age of two, picked up from the trash heap as he whimpered next to his dead mother.

"Father Rick's orphanage amazes me. He has a place there that cares for at least a hundred kids who have no place else to go. Grandma Lavish and I only actually went there in person one time. But I'll always remember what I saw. That whole country is poor. I mean, they have got almost nothing, Christopher. And the orphans don't have *almost* nothing. They've literally got nothing at all. Father Rick's home is their only chance.

"Years ago, he came and spoke at Mass one time at our church and handed out some brochures. Your grandmother and I just wanted to help a little, even when we didn't have much money. That's why we put them in our giving plan like I told you about, and we built up to it. Every year, Father Rick would send us a picture of some of the kids who lived there. Every time I heard about how Jesus had compassion for children, my mind immediately went to Haiti and Father Rick.

"A few years later, Gilbert started to write us letters. He's really smart. And I guess he likes to write. So he wrote us. For years, we never met him. Just got to know him through his little handwritten notes. He loved art. Liked to paint. And he played some soccer. And in his letters, he would describe for us some of the scenery on that little island and some of the interesting people or foods that he discovered.

"Grandma Lavish and I gave the two percent of our giving plan out of my salary to the orphans there. But when those Cascia Cakes really took off, Grandma Lavish decided to make extra gifts each year to the orphanage to help Father Rick pay for school for the kids, so little guys like Gilbert could learn and grow. Gilbert just kind of captured our hearts with his letters.

"Well, he did really well in school. Really, really well, in fact. He was as smart as you, Christopher. And when he finished school, Father Rick wrote us and asked if we could help Gilbert get into a college here in the United States.

"Since I went to Georgia Tech, I knew a few people there. We made some calls and told them about this really smart kid from Haiti who had nothing at all. But we knew he had a good brain, and he had the ability to design stuff and draw it. So Tech decided to give him a chance. Even though he was smart, he needed a lot of help.

"Then Father Rick called us. Believe it or not, he actually found a way to get on the phone and ask us to pay for Gilbert to go to Tech. The nerve of that guy! Get him into college. Now will you pay for it? Your grandmother and I laughed about that one for years. How do you say no to a kid who was found in a trash dump lying next to his dead mother?

"Of course, we said yes. How could we not? Father Rick knew he had us. We loved little Gilbert. But now he's not little anymore. He's a grown man now. Just finished college himself. Has a job in Atlanta and everything.

"When your grandmother died, I called folks to share the news, and I guess word got all the way to Gilbert. Because the next thing I know he's showing up at the funeral. And he's got two other kids from the orphanage who have come to America with him.

"He walks up to me at the cemetery. Introduces me to the other two kids. And then he hands me a photo of his graduation from college. He was wearing a big Georgia Tech Yellow Jacket shirt and had the hugest grin you could imagine. He was so proud.

"Gilbert gave me a hug, and whispered in my ear, 'Thank you. Thank you. You and Lavish. Thank you. I love you so much.'"

When Grandpa finished telling me that, I could barely swallow, the lump in my throat was so big. Grandpa had tears in his eyes, which made me feel a little bit better. I just had never realized all the different kinds of people Grandma Lavish had touched and helped. This was amazing.

I knew that her baking business had done well. And I knew that she had paid for a new Confirmation program to be developed because she wanted young Catholic kids like me to love the faith like she did.

And I knew that LEGS Baking had given a check to St. Catherine's School every month for as long as I've been alive so that any family who wanted their child to go to a Catholic school would not have to worry about how to pay for it. I went to school with a bunch of kids who didn't even know Grandma Lavish but knew that she had paid for their tuition.

Grandma Lavish loved her faith and she loved kids. Of course, she loved me the most. I'm her first grandchild. Who wouldn't love me?! Her best boy. She said so. But she wanted to love kids and help them know Jesus Christ more than anything else.

As I was wiping my face with my hand to get the tears off, Grandpa went inside the house. He quickly came back out and showed me the picture. There was Gilbert, wearing his graduation cap and Yellow Jacket T-shirt, holding up his diploma from Georgia Tech. And the smile. Wow. I will always remember that beaming look on his face. A kid from the trash dump in Haiti who made it through Georgia Tech.

I realized that Father Fisher had been right. I am lucky to be related to Grandma Lavish. She was huge. Just crazy huge. That was why all those people had shown up at her funeral. They were just like Gilbert. Grandma Lavish had touched their lives.

Grandma Lavish liked to say, "God is the Supreme Giver. And when you give, you become just like Him." I guess that means she looks a lot like God.

That picture of Gilbert hit me like an 18-wheeler, because I knew: I'll have big shoes to fill when I grow up. And I still didn't even know where the *S* on the bracelet had come from.

12: THE JALOPY

By the end of that last week of summer, Grandpa was really starting to look tired. He had not been feeling good for a long time. I think he missed Grandma Lavish so much that it just hurt really deep inside. I know it felt like that to me, and he'd known her even longer than I had.

I missed Grandma Lavish too. Talking about her brought her back just a little. Sometimes it was like she was right there with us. But it just wasn't the same. And Grandpa knew it.

On the last Saturday of the summer, right before school started, I asked if I could spend the whole weekend with Grandpa. Mom and Dad didn't mind. They were going somewhere anyway. And Grandpa seemed happy to have me around.

It was the first time I had ever spent the night with just him. I had been there bunches of times when Grandma Lavish was alive. But I had never spent the night at her house without her being there too. That was weird.

I took my sleeping bag. It's a really cool one I got for Christmas back when I was seven or eight. It has all the NFL team helmets on it: Buccaneers, Dolphins, Cowboys, everybody. I liked to put it on the floor next to the bed where Grandpa and Grandma Lavish slept. It was fun to wake up in the morning and see those two curled up on each other in that big old-fashioned bed. Grandma Lavish always got up first. She would slip into the kitchen to start the coffee and get to work on some biscuits. That's what we had for breakfast at my grandparents' house. Every time. Biscuits. And sometimes they let me taste the coffee too. I could count on it, like the sun coming up in the morning.

Anyway, when I got to the house, I put my sleeping bag on the floor where I always did. Then Grandpa asked me if I wanted to go to the hardware store. I noticed that in the months since Grandma Lavish had died, Grandpa liked to get out of the house when he could. I guess it helped him keep his mind off her.

But now we were all getting used to life without Grandma Lavish. And Grandpa wanted to take care of himself as much as he could. He liked to run errands, even when he did not have anything he had to get. He really liked the hardware store. A lot of his friends hung out there, all the other old people.

So we got in his old truck to go to the store. I didn't mind. I got to be with Grandpa. That's what I wanted more than anything else anyway.

Grandpa had driven that 1982 Ford F-150 forever. I had never seen him in any other car. Grandma Lavish drove an old Honda; Grandpa drove his truck. Dad said it had almost two hundred thousand miles on it now. I don't know how far that is, but it sounds really, really big. The bed of that truck looked like an old beat-up washtub, with stains and cracks in it like the ones I saw in yards at garage sales. The red paint had faded in the Florida sun. But Grandpa just kept driving it anyway.

"Grandpa, when did you get this truck anyway?"

"Got it new, Christopher. In 1982. Before you were even born. She's been a good truck, huh?"

"You ever thought about getting a new one?"

"Don't need a new one. She runs fine."

"I was just thinking that it might be nice to have a new truck now."

"Your grandmother and me don't like to spend money on new cars and stuff." Grandpa said. "That's money we could use on something else. We like to keep it simple. Just because she's gone now doesn't mean I am going to change things."

"What are you going to do with Grandma Lavish's Honda?" I asked.

"Haven't given that much thought, Christopher. Why? You got your eye on it? You want to have it for when you turn sixteen and can drive?"

"I don't know, Grandpa. I'm just ten. That's a long way off. I'm not sure that old car will even be around by the time I can drive anyway."

Grandpa just chuckled.

"If you take care of it, Christopher, it will be just fine. Don't waste your money on stuff that goes down in value. Me and Grandma Lavish decided early on to live simple lives. That's where the *S* on the bracelet came from, you know. We wanted to save all we could. Not just save like a savings account like the one your dad set up for you at the bank. But also save money when we bought stuff by not going for all that fancy stuff and luxuries.

"Live on less, Christopher. We knew if we spent less we would always have enough money for what we really needed. And we would be able to give more because we hadn't wasted our money on things that really didn't matter much in the first place. Less is more, Christopher. Remember that after I'm gone."

I sat in the truck and rubbed the bracelet on my wrist while Grandpa drove. I was glad he had brought up the *S*, because we had never talked about that. All summer long, he had told me stories. But never about the *S*.

Grandpa seemed in the mood to talk today. He barely even paused to let me ask questions or say anything. All I had done was just ask about a new truck. He just kept going. Maybe because it was the last Saturday of the summer and he knew I'd get busy with school and all that stuff soon.

As he turned the corner, he said, "Our giving plan was important to us. You saw some of the results for yourself at the funeral. That's why all those folks were there. Because your grandmother had been so generous. People loved her for it. She wanted people to know that she loved them, really know it. And they did. And they loved her right back.

"It was hard to do that giving plan. Ten percent may not sound like a lot to you, Christopher, because you're just ten years old now. But you'll see. When you get older, you are gonna start to want stuff. A new car. A bigger house.

Some nice clothes. A shiny piece of jewelry. A fancy vacation in some exotic place. We decided that wasn't for us. We wanted to be generous. And that meant we could save money by not spending it on crazy stuff that didn't really matter in the first place. God gave us the money, and we decided to use it that way. Like it was His, not ours. We'd rather give our money to help Gilbert go to school than use it on something we would never get back. It's simple, Christopher. Stuff is just stuff. Save all you can.

"Look around, kid. Grandma Lavish is gone. If we had spent all of our money on stuff, I'd be sitting in that house with piles of nice things and have no idea what to do with it all. Surrounded by stuff. Instead, we gave to help people. And I am surrounded by love—all the people we loved and who love us too. Those people make me feel a lot better than looking at some piece of jewelry I don't care about or trying to take care of some big empty house.

"Don't get me wrong. I bought your grandmother a very fine diamond band for our wedding anniversary. And we took some nice trips every now and then so we could have fun and learn some new things. That was my way of showing her how much I loved her. But we tried not to buy crazy stuff. We wanted things that would last and get the job done for a long time.

"So, to answer your question, I'm not gonna get a new truck. Enough about that. You need anything at the hardware store?"

I knew the answer to that one. "Sure, I've been looking at this model car. They have a really cool old Porsche there."

I'd had my eye on that car for a long time, but it cost more than I had. I like to build models in my room. I've done a bunch of them. I keep them on the shelf above my desk.

"We'll see," Grandpa said. That's what he usually said when he wanted to say no but didn't want to hurt your feelings.

Grandpa got quiet and kept driving toward the hardware store.

"Grandpa, can I ask you a question?"

He nodded his head and grunted, "Uh-huh."

"When Grandma Lavish made that first LEGS bracelet, what made her think of the *S* you just mentioned? The *L* for Love came in the prayer chapel. The *E* for Earn came to her when she was studying the Bible at that old neighbor lady's house. And you told me the other day about the *G* and Father Paul's homily and your whole conversation at the restaurant about a giving plan. But what about the *S?* When did Grandma Lavish come up with the *S?*"

Grandpa pulled into the parking lot at the Skillet. I hopped out of the truck and went around to the other side to meet him so we could walk in at the same time. Grandpa was moving slower; I could see that. Everybody could. He just was not the same without Grandma Lavish.

We stepped onto the front porch of the hardware store. Grandpa sat down in a rocking chair there instead of going in. I knew what that meant. Bunches of old people liked to sit on the front porch of the store and talk. I was not gonna get that model Porsche today.

The good news was that nobody else was there on the porch right then. It was just us. Grandpa leaned over and handed me a bunch of quarters and said, "Christopher, go get us a Coke."

I walked over to the machine at the other end of the porch and got him a can of Coke. He liked cans; he said they keep your drink colder than the plastic bottles. I got a Cherry Coke for myself.

When I got back to the chairs, Grandpa began to talk.

"Your grandmother and I never told you about this, Christopher. She didn't like to talk about it much. But she's gone now and you might as well know.

"A couple of years after we got married—I think it was about the time we were thinking about moving back home to Lake Bobola from Orlando—your grandmother got sick. Real sick.

"One evening after supper, she left the room, and headed into the bathroom. And she sat on the toilet for thirty minutes; her insides were cramping so much that she doubled over in pain. Here she was, a young woman, I mean she was just twenty-two or twenty-three years old then, moaning and writhing in pain.

"The next day, things got better and we didn't think much of it. But a few weeks later, her stomach pain and intestinal spasms came back and started to happen almost every day. I don't know if it was her getting stressed out about being married to me, or she hated living in Orlando away from home, or what. Maybe it just ran in her family.

Or maybe we were eating the wrong kind of food or something. Nobody ever really figured it out.

"But finally she went to the doctor. He did some tests, and told us that Grandma Lavish had something called ulcerative colitis. I'd never heard of it before. But I tell you what—it took over her life. Cramping, diarrhea, pain, and bleeding almost every day. She spent the first half hour of the day in the bathroom. Every day. That meant she had to get up at six thirty just to be even with me when I got up at seven.

"Pretty soon, she was making long visits to the bathroom all day long. She almost hated to eat because she knew where it led: more diarrhea and bleeding. Grandma Lavish lost weight and got really skinny and bony. She was tired all the time.

"We tried everything we could think of. Doctors put her on all kinds of medicines. They tried new stuff; they tried old stuff. None of it worked. Somebody told us about a special diet that was supposed to help. We did that for a month or two. Nothing happened.

"The more stuff we tried, the more stressed out she got when it didn't work. The more stressed out she got, the worse off she got. She couldn't do much of anything, Christopher. You know your grandmother. Lots of energy. Always positive and fun. This was the first time she had really ever had to face the fact that her body had limits and that life was not always gonna be happy and smooth.

"She got so bad off that she had to go to the hospital several times just to get fluids because her little body was worn out. One of those times in the hospital, they did this colonoscopy thing they use to check your insides. Grandma Lavish described it to me, but it is just too yucky to talk about, Christopher. Trust me.

"The doctor told us that her large intestine was covered with ulcers. He told her that medications could help, diet might help, and exercise might help too, but ulcerative colitis affected each person differently. One patient might have bad flare-ups one time and never have them show up again. Another person might have flare-ups every so often. And an unlucky few might flare up and never have it ease up at all. For those folks, surgery would be the last resort. Remove the whole colon, and wear a bag for the rest of your life. It was not perfect or painless, but it would be a cure.

"Grandma Lavish suffered. For two years, she fought that stuff. Tried everything the doctors could think of. Special diets. Drugs. Even wore a nicotine patch for a month or two. But no matter what she did, she still went to the bathroom all day long. Lost almost all of her weight. Some of her hair fell out. It was bad.

"There were some days where she lost control of her own body and bowels. She struggled to keep doing the things she liked to do, but it got to be too much. Her days were filled with nerves. She started in the bathroom, and then planned the rest of her day around knowing where the nearest restroom would be. At the grocery store. On the drive to a friend's house. On the way to Mass. Anywhere she went she needed to know where the closest bathroom would be. She just never knew when the urge would come and she would have to find a toilet. It was amazing, really. This woman with all this personality, and beauty, and brains, totally obsessed with having to go to the bathroom. I don't know how she did it.

"The worst day came when she got a bunch of friends together to go shopping. They gathered in the yard at the house so they could ride together in one car. As the friends were jumping into the car, Grandma Lavish felt the urge. She knew she didn't have a choice. She had to get out and sprint back to the house to use that bathroom. Her friends were used to the physical challenges she faced, so they weren't surprised when she popped out of the car and said, 'I'll be right back.'

"They knew. They had seen the panicked look as it swept across her face at any hour of the day and in any situation. We all had seen it. They had prayed for her each day for those two years. So her friends sat in the car and watched your grandmother sprinting from the yard into the house.

"She made it about six or eight steps before it became clear that something was bad wrong. She stopped running right in the middle of the yard. And then she knelt down on the grass beside the pavement by the front steps. And she started to cry.

"Her friends jumped out of the car and ran over to her. There she was: your Grandma Lavish sitting in her own stink, a few yards from the car, and a few more away from her own house. Their beautiful, talented, enthusiastic, and gifted friend was crumpled up in the grass right in front of them, totally broken.

"They called me at work, and I came home. Those two years' physical strain washed all over her. There she sat, embarrassed and humiliated in front of her closest friends, cleaning up her own mess and crying.

"Her friends left. And I sat on the sofa with her the rest of the day. After supper that night, she put her head in my lap and cried. The only thing she could say was, 'Tommy, I'm so humiliated.' She said it over and over again.

"And I told her, 'Lavish, tomorrow you and I need to go see your doctor together. Eight o'clock, right after breakfast. We'll be ready.'

"And we did. We went to see Dr. Bers the next day. He said, 'Lavish, you have actually done better than I expected when I first took a look at your insides. But we've fought this as far as we can go. You are gonna have to have surgery. We'll take out your colon, and you will bounce back. I promise.'"

Grandpa stopped talking and took a drink from his Coke. Two of his friends came up and said hello, and it looked like they were gonna take over the whole conversation. It kind of grossed me out a little bit to talk about this kind of stuff. But I really wanted to know how the story ended.

So I blurted out, "Grandpa, so did she have the surgery? Did she wear that bag you were talking about?

I braced myself for him to give me that scowl he makes when he's not happy or for him to say something quick and rude to tell me to shut up. But this time was different. Grandpa told his friends that he and I were having a man-to-man talk that he needed to get back to, and he started talking again.

"Christopher, she had the surgery. A couple of weeks after she messed all over herself and her dress in front of her friends in her own yard. They opened her up, and took out all of her large intestine. The surgeon showed me the whole thing just so I could see for myself how it was covered with sores. When I saw that, it made me hurt inside for just how much pain my precious wife had been carrying. Seeing it made it real.

"Anyway, she was in the hospital for almost a week. And that's where the *S* came from, since you asked. It came in the hospital.

"While she was there, I had to work most of the time. So she was by herself a lot. But a nun was one of the main chaplains at the hospital there in Orlando, and she would come by to see her. Except she didn't just pop in and visit and then move on. No, the nun would come in, and sit down and say nothing. A lot of the time Grandma Lavish was asleep, and the sister wouldn't wake her up. Just sit down and read a newspaper or a book sitting in the chair there next to her. Your grandmother told me that that was the greatest gift she got. Just that nun's presence. Not trying to tell her anything or make her talk or entertain. The sister was just there. She was never in a rush. Just quietly sitting beside her. And knowing that made her feel really comfortable and safe.

"Well, the third day was the hardest. It always is, after surgery. The pain has set in, the anesthesia is working its way out of your body; it's just a hard day. But on the fourth day, she was lying there on her back in the hospital bed, and the nun was sitting next to her. Sister Diane, I think her name was.

"Grandma Lavish asked her to pray for her. So she did. And she said that what happened when the nun prayed was a lot like that day in the prayer chapel before we got married, when she was staring at the crucifix and all of a sudden was overwhelmed. Father Cascia, and Jesus, and the presence of God all just overwhelmed her. Remember when I told you about that?"

"Uh-huh."

"Well, something like that happened again. I wasn't there because I was at work. But what she told me was that Sister Diane was praying, and her words were just floating through the room. And the whole time Sister Diane was staring at the big incision wound on your grandmother's belly as she prayed. An intense, warm feeling covered her whole body as the nun stared at the stitches.

"When she finished the prayer, the sister told her that she saw that wound on her belly and it looked like a crucifix. Like Jesus was stretched out on the cross right there on her stomach where the stitches and staples were. And Sister Diane said she knew that God was somehow touching your grandmother with His hand, like it was actually stretching right down from heaven into the hospital room and onto that wound. And your Grandma Lavish said she could feel Him right there. He was nearer to her in this surgery and suffering than ever before.

"When Sister Diane stood up to leave, the room grew quiet, and your grandmother told her, 'Thank you. Thank you for coming. Thank you for sitting with me. Thank you for praying. And most of all, thank you for sharing about the crucifix on my wound and the hand of God. All of that. Thank you.'

"As she left the room, Sister Diane told her, 'Lavish, I'm really happy for you. I know nuns in convents and monasteries who spend their whole lives waiting and hoping to have a moment like we just shared. Where God is so close and so real. We're blessed.'

"And then she was gone."

Grandpa paused again, drank some more Coke. He put the can to his face and stared at me. He was weird like that. Things didn't gross him out like they did me. He could sit at the dinner table and talk about getting his tooth pulled or an opossum he had run over in the middle of the highway and not think a thing about it. So talking about Grandma Lavish's belly wound didn't seem to bother him a bit, even if we were sitting on the front porch of the hardware store.

I didn't know what to say. Here was this amazing story about Grandma Lavish that no one had ever told me before. And I never knew about it. She had been wearing a bag on her belly my whole life and nobody ever even told me.

Grandpa swallowed and kept going. He was in a zone or something. It was like he was gonna talk all day.

"Now, about that *S.*"

I nodded and waited.

"I guess it was the colitis and the humiliation. Maybe your grandmother realized that she could have died from all that. Life is short, Christopher. Then the surgery. Then she had that nun tell her about the hand of God and the crucifix on her stomach. And she felt something about the cross and the crucifixion and the suffering of Jesus. I never could quite put my finger on exactly how that whole time affected her.

"But when she got home from the hospital, Grandma Lavish told me she didn't care about stuff anymore. The suffering had changed her. She said I never needed to worry again about her wanting to move to a bigger house or hoping to go on some big vacation. The pain and the tubes and the blood somehow had helped her discover that this life was brief and temporary, but eternity would be, well, forever. Having stuff just didn't matter. Said she had tasted the forever presence of God and couldn't turn back to this world and silly stuff like cars and rings and shoes. She wanted to live a simple life, not an extravagant one.

"I noticed it about her. She really didn't care about things after the colitis and surgery and the crucifix. I think somehow the suffering made her purer. She was already special. But now she was even more different. She really cared even more about love, if you can believe that. And she cared more about God.

"It's kind of hard to describe, Christopher. We didn't talk about her suffering much together. You'd think we would have discussed it lots of times over the years, but we didn't. And we sure never brought it up with other people. None of their business, really. But that's where the *S* came from. Save all you can. Don't spend all your money on stuff. Simple is better. She really believed that, and it helped her love people all the more. She and I decided to save money by living simply. That way, we could give more."

I knew Grandpa was telling me the truth. Grandma Lavish loved simple things. When she saw my mom looking at fancy stuff one time in a store, Grandma Lavish told her that Jesus was born in a feed bin and rode on a donkey. He never even had a home. So Grandma Lavish wanted to be lavish in her giving but not in her living. She was going to live simply so she could give boldly. Like she told me a thousand times, "I want people to really know that I love them." *Save all you can.*

Grandpa kept talking as he wiped his mouth. "She meant it. She really did. And that's why so many people showed up when she died."

We finished our talk, and rode back to Grandpa's house. We never even went into the hardware store. I didn't mind not getting that model Porsche. We had a great night. We sat in the swing, we talked, and we watched the moon fill up the sky.

I dreaded school starting, so I stayed up as late as Grandpa would let me. I wanted that night to last forever. But it didn't.

13: THE VISIT

Now you know where that bracelet came from. And how Grandma Lavish came up with the idea for the letters. LEGS. But I almost forgot to tell you how I got it. You really need to know that for this all to make sense.

I still remember the day; I always will. It was back before summer started, during the last week of school. That week when you're not doing a lot at school anyway. Did you ever have one of those teachers who showed a lot of movies and had some parties on the last days before summer? They're great.

Anyway, on Thursday, after lunch, our PE teacher, Coach Owenby, was leading all of us ten-year-old boys in learning and practicing the full-court pressure defense he loved so much. He called it 40 Minutes of Hell, just like his favorite basketball coaches, Nolan Richardson and Rick Pitino, did.

Around two o'clock, Mom walked through the door of the gym. I knew right then that something was up. Mom never showed up at school. I rode my bike to and from school; she didn't take me. The only times I saw her at school were for teacher conferences or when she had to check me out early to go to the dentist or something.

Well, Mom walked in and waved at me to come over. Then she told me that the rest of our family was out in the car waiting. I needed to check out of school and leave now.

I picked up my gym bag, then I went to my class and got my backpack, and told my teacher that Mom was here to check me out early. Mom and I went to the office and signed out, and scooted out to the parking lot to jump in the van. I was surprised to see two of my cousins and my aunt Jenny in the van too. My head began to spin. What in the world was going on? Mom handed me a pair of pants, a dress shirt, and a sport coat. She mumbled, "Put this on."

Nobody was saying anything so I spit it out: "What's going on? Where are we going?"

Mom said, "Just get dressed, son. We'll be there soon enough."

Michael was in the seat next to me. He was playing some game where he yelled out the letters of the alphabet when he saw them on road signs. Really annoying. He didn't know what was going on either.

I knew the roads. We'd driven this way hundreds of times.

Seven people in the van, and Mom and Dad said next to nothing. Dad drove the van through the familiar neighborhoods of Lake Bobola. He just fiddled with his watch, like he really needed to know what time it was or something.

Finally, he pulled the car into the driveway and turned off the engine. He got out of the van and waved at everyone else to fall in line behind him. Dad walked up to the door of the house and gently knocked. A chubby lady

I had never seen before opened the door, saying, "Come on in. She's been expecting you." She was wearing clothes like those people who work in hospitals on the TV shows Grandpa liked to watch.

Dad asked, "Is she ready for us?"

The chubby lady nodded.

Dad told Mom and Aunt Jenny, "You wait here. She wants to see the boys and me alone."

Dad took my hand and Michael's and then motioned to my two cousins, Steven and Thomas, to follow along. We made our way down the hall to the second door on the right.

Dad stepped in first. Then the four of us followed closely behind him. The bedroom was tiny, with barely enough room for the four of us to stand next to the small twin bed tucked against the wall. Grandma Lavish lay in the bed, her eyes weak, her hair like a bird's nest. She opened her eyes and whispered, "Leave the boys here. Go be with your wife and sister."

Following directions, Dad made his way back to the kitchen, leaving Steven, Thomas, Michael, and me alone in the room with Grandma Lavish, who clearly was not doing well. Only a few years before, this wonderful woman had stood 5'4" with bright eyes and a healthy body. Now she lay all shrunk up and curled in the small bed. Cancer had eaten her body right before our eyes.

Staring at us with her weak, gray eyes, Grandma Lavish said, "Are you ready? I want to say something and I want you to write it down. Ready?"

We looked at each other, confused. None of us knew what to do. Since I was the oldest, I searched the room for a few scraps of paper and pencils. When I found them on the little desk in the corner, I handed some to Michael, Steven, and Thomas. We all stood still and stared back at the dying woman in the bed.

Grandma Lavish said again, "Are you ready?"

"We are," we said together. "Yes ma'am."

"Good, because I want you to write this down."

"Yes ma'am."

"Are you ready to write it down now?"

"Yes ma'am," we insisted again.

"OK," she said slowly, "here it is."

We leaned in to be near her as she lay struggling.

Grandma Lavish cleared her throat and sat up slightly in the bed.

The words came out quickly but clearly. "Always remember who you are."

I scribbled that on the scrap of paper.

Then my worn-out grandmother motioned to me with her finger to come closer to her. I stood next to her. She raised her right hand a little and took my hand in hers. When she squeezed my hand, I realized that in the palm of her hand was the little bracelet that she had always worn. Her LEGS bracelet.

Grandma Lavish was giving me the bracelet. She looked at me and said nothing. She just nodded and smiled weakly as her eyes focused on mine. I knew. The bracelet belonged to me now.

She closed her eyes, making it clear that that was all she had to say to us and that we could leave. I put the bracelet on my left wrist and rubbed it with my fingers. I didn't know what to say.

Just then, Grandpa stepped into the room. When he saw that I was wearing Grandma Lavish's special bracelet, he took my wrist and pressed it to his chest. His eyes filled up with tears. He said nothing, and we quickly left the room to go find my father.

"Always remember who you are."

She had looked at me, my brother, and my cousins and said, "Always remember who you are." I wanted to remember those words.

Later that day, Grandma Lavish was gone. And I had held her hand just before she died. Those were the last words my grandmother would ever say to me. And she said them just before I touched her warm body for the last time.

I put that bracelet on that day, and I don't ever want to take it off again. It reminds me of life's greatest lesson.

14: TODAY

Even though I am a grown man now, I still wear that bracelet. Each day, when I wake up in the morning, I rub my fingers over it and remember.

As the first grandson of Tom and Lavish Grace, I have big shoes to fill. They knew the most important thing. Life's greatest lesson.

Grandma Lavish called it LEGS.

Love all you can.

Earn all you can.

Give all you can.

Save all you can.

Grandma Lavish's special bracelet, her legacy. A Lavish legacy, I like to call it. The best way to live. The only way, really, if you want your life to matter. Love generously and your life will be filled with love in return. Give generously and you will always be blessed.

I still live in Lake Bobola. That's home for me, just like it was for my parents and my grandparents before me. There's nothing super special about the place, I suppose, but it's home. And that's what matters to me.

When I wear the bracelet, it sparks a lot of good conversations. Some folks still remember my Grandma Lavish and want to talk about her. Other people like to ask me about LEGS Baking and whether it is still operating. It is. But best of all, at least twice a week, someone asks me, "Why in the world are you wearing a bracelet with the word LEGS on it?" And then I have the opportunity to share her Lavish legacy with someone else. I tell them about LEGS and my faith, and about how my grandparents loved me enough to want me to become the-best-version-of-myself. They wanted me to have a purpose and a mission. Living by LEGS does just that. It really is life's greatest lesson.

Grandma Lavish was right. If you can just do that, you will have lived well. Because you will have loved well. And you will have embraced God. After all, He made you in the first place for just that purpose. I saw it with my own eyes in Grandpa and Grandma Lavish. They loved completely. They were the happiest people I've ever known. All the people at her funeral proved that.

When Grandma Lavish was gone, I missed her something awful, but you already know that. I knew then that I wanted to grow up to be just like her and Grandpa. They taught me to be generous and to love all I could.

They wrote down their giving plan every year, usually after Christmas, sometime before each new year started. Not long after Grandma Lavish died, I made my own giving plan. I wrote it down just like she and Grandpa had done after they heard Father Paul's message about the widow's mite and Grandma Lavish had read the magazine article about Robbie Russell. The time when they sketched out their first plan over lunch after Mass.

Even though I was just ten years old, I wrote down my first giving plan on a piece of notebook paper. I set the same goal my grandparents had of growing toward giving ten percent of my money to help other people each year.

I still have that very first giving plan. Here's what it looked like:

The Christopher Grace
Giving Plan

1998: 1% to St. Catherine's
      Parish Youth
1999: 2% to St. Catherine's Youth
2000: 3% to St. Catherine's Youth
2001: 4% to St. Catherine's Youth
2002: 5% to St. Catherine's Youth
2003: 6% = 5% to St. Catherine's
      Youth + 1% to Orphans in Haiti
2004: 7% = 5% to St. Catherine's
      Youth + 2% to Orphans in Haiti
2005%: 8% = 5% to St. Catherine's
      Youth + 3% to Orphans in Haiti
2006: 9% = 5% to St. Catherine's Youth
      + 4% to Orphans in Haiti
2007: 10% = 5% to St. Catherine's
      Youth + 5% to Orphans in Haiti

I wanted to be the person Grandma Lavish wanted me to be and the person God wanted me to be. I decided that the two ministries that were most important in my life were my home parish, St. Catherine's, and the orphanage Grandpa and Grandma Lavish had helped. The one where Gilbert had grown up.

So I started giving right then, at age ten. I made money cutting grass in my neighborhood and even did a few projects to help my baseball coach improve our field. He paid me some for that. And, of course, I worked a day or two here and there at LEGS Baking. Partly to make a little money but mostly to remember my grandmother and to feel a little closer to her.

Grandpa was right. The giving was fun. In fact, it gave me so much joy that I got to my ten percent goal in three years, when I was thirteen, rather than in the ten years I had planned at the start. I guess I was like Grandpa in that way. It was hard at first, but once I got started, it became fun, even at the age of ten. And there I was, following in the footsteps of my grandmother, trying to keep up with her. It really was a lot easier than I had thought.

But it got harder. By the time I was sixteen, I had discovered cars. And then I discovered girls. And then I went off to college. I never realized when I was ten how many other things I could spend money on. In high school and college, I sure found out! And I am sad to tell you that my giving plan disappeared. For several years there, in college, I didn't even write one down at the start of the year. I still gave a dollar here and there to a homeless man on the street or a kid collecting door-to-door for the food pantry. Other than that, I believed my money was mine and I was gonna use it how I wanted to. I knew I worked hard for that money. And I felt entitled to spend it how I wanted. I didn't care about God or other people.

For a time in my life, a giving plan just seemed like something old and fuddy-duddy. Like something sappy you do when you're a little kid or when you're real old like my Grandma Lavish. I thought I was smarter than all that. That giving plan became something that my grandparents did way back in the old days, but it had nothing to do with me now. It was too restrictive for a free young man like me. I was going to be bold and free. I guess you could say I forgot who I was.

After I graduated from college, I got my first job and lived on my own. That felt good too—freedom. I could do whatever I wanted and be whoever I wanted to be. I was free. Or at least that's what I thought.

And then I started dating Rita.

She'd grown up in Florida like I had, so we had lots in common. Like me, she was Catholic. Unlike me, she actually went to Mass and paid attention to God in her life.

Rita and I had been dating a few months when I knew. It was obvious—she was the one for me. I'm not sure how you know, but you just do. And I did. We began to see each other more often, and I soon knew where this relationship was headed.

As we became more serious about each other, I told her I wanted her to visit my grandparents' graves with me in the cemetery here in Lake Bobola. So one evening, when it was cooler outside, we walked down to the cemetery at St. Catherine's church. I showed her around that old place.

Rita asked me, "Is this the church you grew up in?"

I answered, "Yes. I never told you that before?" I was a little surprised I had never even mentioned it. Embarrassed, really.

"No, sweetie. I knew you were Catholic, but you don't show it much." She chuckled a little at that one. But she was right. I didn't show it much. In fact, I probably didn't show it at all, if you know what I mean.

"I've been trying to figure out how to get you to start going to Mass with me. If we are ever going to have a future together, Christopher, faith needs to be a part of who we are. Together. Now that I know this place means something to you, you just made my job a lot easier." She smiled. But that smile made me a little nervous.

"What do you mean?" I asked.

"Well, you talk about your grandparents all the time. And if they are buried here, and this was your parish as a kid, you need to be here. We will come here together. OK?"

I just nodded my head.

She was right. I had wandered. I knew it too. I had forgotten who I was and what I was made of. Most of my friends had done the same thing, so I really had not given it a second thought. Church, Mass, God, all that stuff just had not seemed very important over the past few years. But Rita was important to me, and faith was important to her, so faith was going to be important to me too. She was right, and I knew it.

Plus, I knew that I knew better anyway. Grandma Lavish and Grandpa had built the faith into me. I had just chosen to have spiritual amnesia for a few years.

Rita and I walked through the St. Catherine's cemetery that evening. And when we came up on the gravestones for my grandparents, I pointed at them and proudly read aloud the words inscribed on Grandma Lavish's tombstone.

Those words opened the door for me to share with Rita the most important parts of my life. Grandma Lavish. Grandpa. The bracelet. LEGS. Strawberry cakes. Officer Harry Beasley. Gilbert. The giving plan. And my faith.

I laid it all out there for her; showed her everything inside me. I hadn't realized just how much stuff I was carrying around inside that I had never shared with the woman I loved. I think she knew when we left the cemetery that night that our lives would be together from then on. By seeing those gravestones and asking about my Grandma Lavish, Rita had helped me remember who I really was. It was like I had run away from myself for a few years, but the real me was home now. And it was nice to discover that, believe it or not, Rita actually liked the real me.

When we got back to my home that night, Rita made me sit down right then and there and sketch out a giving plan.

"You've been raised right. You have a purpose: LEGS. It's time to embrace that, Christopher. It's time. Let's do this together," she told me.

She was right, you know. But like Grandpa had done with Grandma Lavish, now I was running to catch up with the girl I loved. She just always seemed to be a few steps ahead of me when it came to the things that mattered. I suspect Grandpa and Grandma Lavish got a good chuckle out of watching that.

So together Rita and I sat down at the kitchen table. I have Grandma Lavish's table in my own little kitchen in Lake Bobola. That's the one piece of furniture that I still have from my grandmother's house. Rita and I mapped out a plan on that table for me to begin giving the way I was made and intended for.

I wish I could have sat in Grandpa's old brown recliner when we were done, but when we divided up my grandparents' belongings, each of the grandchildren got to pick just one piece. I chose Grandma Lavish's kitchen table. My cousin Thomas chose that recliner. Maybe I'll buy it from him one day. I'd love to figure out a way to move into my grandparents' house and raise my family there. And wouldn't it be great if I could have Grandma Lavish's kitchen table right there in the middle of her old kitchen, and Grandpa's chair nestled near the TV? I'd love it. Maybe one day.

But at that kitchen table, Rita and I wrote down my new giving plan. I set a goal of ten percent. That had worked for Grandma Lavish, Father Paul had suggested it, and I had actually accomplished it by the time I was thirteen. I knew I could add more than one percent a year and get to my goal of ten percent more quickly than my grandparents had—I had already done that too when I was a kid. I knew from experience how good it feels to be generous, so my new plan got me to the goal in just four years instead of ten.

Rita and I decided to keep it simple for now. We would focus our giving first on the two ministries that inspired us the most: St. Catherine's parish and Father Rick's orphanage in Haiti. In fact, we decided to make a trip to Haiti every year so we could really feel like we were a part of that special work.

Here's the plan that we wrote down that night. It became what Rita and I still do together.

The Christopher Grace
Family Giving Plan

2012:	2% to St. Catherine's Parish
2013:	5% to St. Catherine's Parish
2014:	5% to St. Catherine's Parish
	+ 3% to Orphans in Haiti
2015:	5% to St. Catherine's Parish
	+ 5% to Orphans in Haiti

You probably noticed that I wrote "The Christopher Grace Family Giving Plan" this time. That's because Rita and I have been married for a year now.

We've been to Haiti twice. Father Rick has passed away, but his work goes on and is led by a terrific priest named Father Sean. We love him.

On our last trip there we became friends with a ten-year-old girl named Marie. She lives in the older kids' section of the home.

One night, over dinner, she told Rita and me her story.

"My dad left us when I was two or three. I barely remember him, but I miss him. He was my dad, you know? All I remember is that we were really hungry after he left. Always hungry. And Mom worked and worked to find food for my brothers and me. A fatherless family with four kids and a mom. It was hard.

"We would have a small bowl of rice and beans once a day. That was all the food we could afford. Most nights, I fell asleep with an empty stomach. After I got tired of thinking how hungry I was, I would finally go to sleep.

"When I was little, Mom dropped us off at another orphanage. She was worn out and just couldn't do it anymore. Some folks said that she had AIDS, but I don't believe it. But it really doesn't matter. We had no shoes, we had only rags to wear, and we knew that we would never be able to go to school.

"I've only seen her one time since then. But that was a few years ago. So I guess she's dead now.

"That other orphanage was run by a bunch of really mean folks. We thought our life was gonna be better, but it wasn't. We got a pair of shoes, but anytime we got in trouble, the big man in charge would take them back. He beat us. All the time, he would hit you and yell at you. And we still only had a little rice and beans to eat.

"I don't know how it happened but somebody must have called the government. Because one day, a bunch of people in uniforms came in and told us to get all of our stuff, that we were moving. That's when they brought us here. To Father Sean and the people here. The people closed that other place down. I guess because it was so bad.

"I remember the look on Father Sean's face when we came up. He looked worried. He told the men in the uniforms that he wanted to help but didn't have the money or the rooms. The uniform men told him he had to decide right then. The other place was closed, and this was the best choice. If Father Sean would not take my brothers and me, and the six other kids from the bad guy, the uniformed men would just take us someplace else.

"Thank God Father Sean said yes. I don't know how he did it, but he got people to give the money to feed us too. And now we get to go to school. My brothers and I are way behind. Math is hard. But at least we are learning.

"Thank you for coming to visit us. And thank you for helping Father Sean."

As we sat with little Marie, I wept. Tears of sadness for this little girl whose life had been so hard. Tears of gratitude for people like Father Sean, who gives all he has to help.

And tears of joy that Rita and I get to be a small part of that in addition to what we do in our parish.

Over the years, what started as Father Rick's little orphanage operating on a shoestring has grown from serving seven children to now housing, educating, and loving eighty-two children, with Father Sean at the helm. My grandparents were a big part of that growth. And now Rita and I are pouring ourselves into that same work of love. Pretty cool.

When Marie was telling us her story, I had this deep, warm feeling way down inside of me. I realized that, thanks to Rita, I am filling Grandma Lavish's shoes in a way. Loving. Giving. And that warm feeling was like a smile, Grandma Lavish's smile from heaven, filling my belly with her delight just like the bowl of chicken soup and the math book beside her place mat were filling the belly of little Marie.

If it hadn't been for Rita, I'm not sure how long it would have taken me to remember who I was.

Very soon, we'll be welcoming our first child. The doctors say it will be a girl.

I can't wait to meet her. And to watch her eat her first bite of strawberry cake. We're gonna call her Lavish.

And I bet you already know who will be the next wearer of that special bracelet. The one with the letters: LEGS.

THE INVITATION

To the Reader:

I pray that this story has been helpful and inspiring to you. While names and details have all been changed, most of the stories are true. I know because they have occurred in my own life.

My hope is that this story will move you to discover your own passion and purpose. May you pursue that with generosity . . . and with LEGS.

Grace and Peace,

Allen R. Hunt

THE PLAN

How to Live Lavish's Legacy: the LEGS Model

1) Decide to love generously.

> This is what you are made for. Love all you can. Maybe even get a LEGS bracelet to wear to remind you of your purpose. You might consider having a generosity coach—someone you know who is generous and will spend time with you to help you grow forward and to hold you accountable along the way.

2) Establish a giving plan.

> **First**, *look at your checking account records or your tax returns to determine what percentage of your income you give away now.* Include and add up each transaction of what you gave away over the past year. Now divide that number by your total income for the past year. Write that percentage down next to this year's date. This is what you give now.

> **Second**, *set a giving goal for each coming year that grows that figure by one percent a year until it reaches ten percent of your income sometime in the future.* For example if you give two percent now, set a goal of three percent for next year, four percent for the year after that, and

so on until you reach ten percent. Taking small steps toward a greater goal is the surest way to achieve your big goal.

Third*, pray and discuss the ministries or efforts that are most inspiring and important to you.* Focus your giving and its impact by concentrating on the three or four ministries most meaningful to you. Consider making your parish the first priority, since it is your spiritual home base and the community that sustains and encourages you.

Fourth*, write down those three or four ministries next to each of the years* on your plan and determine how much you plan to give to each of them in the coming years. Remember, you can always adjust the ministries and allocations as you live into the plan in the coming days and years. But it is important to have a written plan so that you have a target to aim for. Setting a goal and writing it down dramatically increases the likelihood that you will achieve it.

Fifth*, share your plan with at least one other person* (family member, spouse, close friend, your priest) so that he or she can hold you accountable from time to time. Sharing your plan with another person makes it real and significantly increases the likelihood of your fulfilling it. Pray. Ask God to help you and bless your giving as you seek to fulfill your plan.

Visit **DYNAMICCATHOLIC.COM/GIVINGPLAN**

1) Get Allen's free worksheet
to help you develop your own giving plan.

&

2) Take a look at five other
people's own real life giving plans.

Let us use this world's goods as we ought,
in order that we may readily receive
those of the world to come.

SAINT JOHN CHRYSOSTOM

NOTES

NOTES